WAL

in the

KENDAL AREA

Series 2 – 2nd Edition

Published by
the Kendal Group
of the
Ramblers' Association

"The Ramblers' Association promotes
rambling, protects rights of way,
campaigns for access to open country
and defends the beauty
of the countryside."

Further information can be obtained from:
The Ramblers, 1/5 Wandsworth Road, London SW8 2XX
Telephone: 01-582 6878

Registered Charity Number 306089

ISBN 0 904350 34 7

Barbon

FOREWORD

This is a new and retitled edition of our second book of walks in the Kendal area. It has been fully revised and brought up to date. Again, we have concentrated on clear and precise directions for routefinding; we make no apologies for including only a little additional information, enabling us to keep down the size and the cost of the booklet.

Please read the directions carefully, and be sure to follow the Country Code printed overleaf. This is very much a sheep and cattle rearing area, and it is essential to keep dogs on leads at all times. Hay and silage for winter feeding are produced in many fields, and it is important not to trample the growing crops (though where the line of a path crosses a field you should follow it in single file rather than going round the edge).

If you meet any difficulties not mentioned in the text, please be so good as to inform the editor at the address given below, giving the date, the exact place (ideally with grid reference), and precise nature of the problem. All routes are on rights of way, except where otherwise stated.

Bus services are very limited these days, but where there is the possibility of using one we have mentioned it. For information about local bus services, visit the Tourist Information Centre at Kendal Town Hall, or call Cumbria County Council Travel Link on 0228-812812.

All the walks except No. 15 are circular and therefore ideal for car travellers.

You should be able to follow the routes without additional maps, but we strongly recommend that you use one if possible, as it will greatly increase your enjoyment and enable you to discover more paths or to adapt these walks to your special needs. The following Ordnance Survey maps cover the walks in this book:

Outdoor Leisure 7: The English Lakes South Eastern Area (for walks nos. 2, 3, 4, 6 (part), 7, 10, 13, 14, and 15)

Pathfinder 617: Sedbergh & Baugh Fell (for part of walk no. 12

Pathfinder 627: Milnthorpe (for walks nos. 1, 5 (part), 6 (part), 8, 9 (part), 11, and 18 (part)

Pathfinder 628: Kirkby Lonsdale & Barbon (for walks nos. 9 (part), 12 (part), 17, and 18 (part)

Pathfinder 637: Burton-in-Kendal & Caton (for walks nos. 16 and 18 (part)

Pathfinder 636: Grange-over-Sands (for part of walk no. 5)

The Kendal Group of the Ramblers' Association

Editor – Margaret Adams, 6 Riverbank Road, Kendal, Cumbria LA9 5JS

Key to Map Starting Points

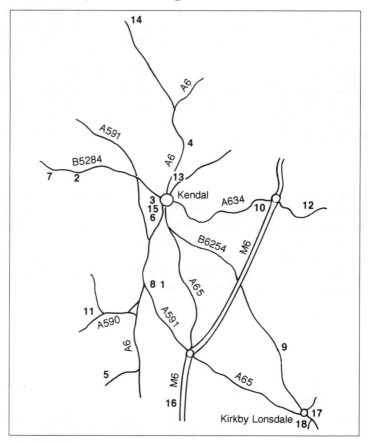

THE COUNTRY CODE
Enjoy the countryside and respect its life and work
Guard against all risk of fire
Fasten all gates except where the farm has left them open
Keep your dogs under close control
Keep to public paths across farmland
Use gates and stiles to cross fences, hedges and walls
Leave livestock, crops and machinery alone
Take your litter home
Help to keep all water clean
Protect wildlife, plants and trees
Take special care on country roads
Make no unnecessary noise

Contents

		km	miles	page
1	Sedgwick to Stainton	6.4	4	6
2	A round from Crook	6.4	4	9
3	Cunswick Scar	8.0	5	11
4	The Watchgate Moraine	8.8	5½	14
5	Haverbrack Bank and the Fairy Steps	8.8	5½	17
6	Helsington Barrows and Scout Scar	8.8	5½	20
7	Around Gilpin Beck	8.8	5½	22
8	Sizergh Castle or Brigsteer Woods and the River Kent	10.4	6½	25
9	Two Meres Walk	12.0	7½	30
10	Roan Edge and Docker Fell	10.4	6½	32
11	Whitbarrow	10.4	6½	35
12	Killington	12.8	8	38
13	River Mint and the Flanks of Benson Knott	13.6	8½	42
14	Three Passes Walk	16.0	10	45
15	Kendal to Bowness-on-Windermere via Underbarrow	16.8	10½	47
16	Hutton Roof Crag and the Lancaster Canal	18.4	11½	52
17	The Seven Churches of Kirkby Lonsdale (1)	19.2	12	55
18	The Seven Churches of Kirkby Lonsdale (2)	18.4	11½	60

Maps*, drawings and cover photo by David Walsh

*Maps based on O.S. Pathfinder Series with the permission of HM Stationery Office

Walk No. 1

SEDGWICK TO STAINTON   minimum 6.4km (4 miles)

Parts of this walk, including an optional detour to Crooklands, follow the towpath of the disused Kendal and Lancaster canal, which passes through the village of Sedgwick. The old canal is being cared for by the Lancaster Canal Trust, which aims to reopen it one day as a waterway for leisure use, in spite of enormous obstacles like the M6. Meanwhile it has become a haven for wildlife, and the number of flowers is increasing year-by-year. There are fine views from the high points on the return route.

At Sedgwick you can reach the towpath by a flight of stone steps on the west side of the aqueduct in the centre of the village (GR 514870). The walk goes in a south-westerly direction for about 400m (¼ mile) to a bridge, beyond which there is no sign of the canal. Cross the field,

Walk 1

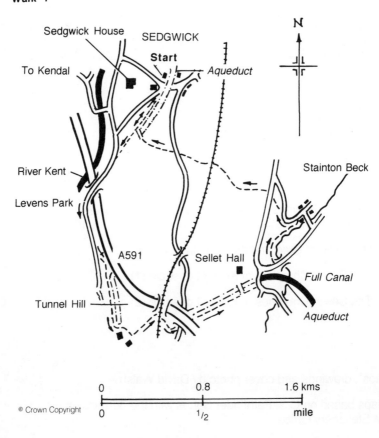

0 — 0.8 — 1.6 kms

0 — 1/2 — mile

passing close to the right-hand one of two oak trees ahead until, after the second electricity pole, you see a signposted stile on the right in a corner of the field. The stile leads to a bridge over the A591 trunk road.

Cross the bridge and follow the lane past the east entrance of Levens Park. About 800m (½ mile) from the bridge, a signposted gap in the hedge on the left leads back to the towpath. Follow the towpath until it swings left towards the mouth of the canal tunnel, where an explanatory notice gives some of the history of the canal.

Find the old horse path on the right of the tunnel and follow this bridleway round to the left and over the top of the hill. After about 350m (¼ mile) you reach the railway line, where the sunken track turns right and passes under the line to regain the towpath where the horses used to rejoin the barges.

The towpath is soon cut again by the A591. Turn left along the lane under the main road to rejoin the towpath via a stile on the right immediately after the underpass. Follow the towpath again, past Sellet Hall bridge and on to the next bridge, where a stile between gates leads out to a lane. From this point there is water in the canal

You could follow the canal for another two miles to Crooklands, where you can get meals at the Crooklands Hotel. If you are less ambitious (or less affluent), cross the canal on the road and turn right into the hamlet of Stainton. Just past the first house, a signpost on the right points to Stainton Bridge End; you could make a minor detour here to see the Stainton beck passing under another aqueduct, and perhaps to picnic beside the beck beyond the aqueduct. The path starts beside the garage on the right of the facing cottage at the bottom of the drive; it can be very wet after heavy rain.

To continue the walk, follow the lane past the signpost and, just before the bridge over the beck, go through an iron field gate on the left. Bear right after a few metres (before the next field gate) across some waste ground and over a double stile leading to another field. Continue beside the hedge on the left to a gap in the corner, and then follow the hedge on the right to the far side of the field, where there is a stone stile close to a small beck.

Over the stile turn left along the lane to where there is a stile on the left about 100m beyond the bend. Cross the stile, go diagonally up the steep bank, and then aim for the signpost that marks a stile at the far side of the field. Here cross the lane, go through a gate opposite and down by the hedge to a ladder stile at the bottom of the field. Continue along the edge of the field to the corner fence post, then aim half right to another stile in the hedge on the right. Over this stile, keep in the same direction through a field gate and onto the railway crossing (marked by a warning notice). Cross the line with great care, and go up the field beside the hedge and over the hill to Wellheads Lane.

Hincaster Tunnel

Cross the lane to an iron kissing gate, and continue climbing, aiming for the mature trees ahead. After passing between the trees, aim for the left end of a line of trees at the bottom of the field, which marks the course of the old canal. Here go through the gate and cross the bridge to the towpath. Turn right to retrace your steps to Sedgwick.

Walk No. 2

A ROUND FROM CROOK   6.4km (4 miles)

Although this pleasant pastoral walk in the National Park is never very far from the main road through Crook, there are some fine views, and the walk is ideal for a sunny summer evening.

You can park by the start at GR 453951 on the B5284 Kendal to Bowness road, just west of Crook Memorial Hall. Take care not to block the gateways and turning circles.

Cross the ladder stile on the north side of the road, close to the drive to Yew Tree Farm, and bear right to a wall with a stile between two gates. Continue diagonally across the next field to cross a stile in the far corner. Now follow the wall on the left to a ladder stile. Over the stile, turn sharp left through a gateway and continue to follow a wall on the left and cross another stile. On joining a farm track, follow it right towards Crook End.

Just before the buildings, go through a kissing gate on the left and follow the waymarks up beside the walls on the left, ignoring the first gateway, to reach another ladder stile. The right of way ahead, beside the wall, may be overgrown with gorse bushes; it is more rewarding to find a way through the bushes to the top of the hill on the right, where a cairn marks a fine view in all directions.

Descend the hill to the right of way, which goes through a kissing gate to the farmyard at Yew Tree Farm. Go down the yard and through another kissing gate on the right at the head of the drive. Continue across the field to another stile leading onto a concrete drive. Follow this towards Field Tenement, but just before the farm go through an iron hand gate on the left and continue below the curtilage wall and across the field to a wooden step stile.

Bear right over a small beck, from where the path passes close to the back of Box Tree Cottage and past the end of the barn to another stile. Now keep beside the wall on the left around two sides of the field to a gap in the far corner, and continue to follow a wall on the left to pass above the next buildings at Sunnybrow. After crossing the next wall stile, with its steep flight of steps, go through the second gateway and diagonally down the field to a kissing gate in the far corner. Turn left to reach the B5284 again.

Walk 2

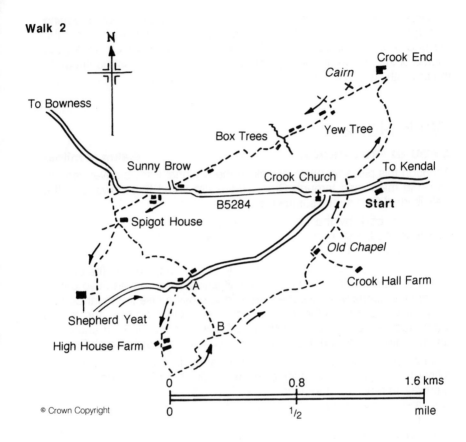

Turn right along the road for 200m, passing two driveways on the left, after which cross another stile on the left beside a gate. This place was once the site of a Friends' meeting house, but all that remains is the small enclosure on the left, formerly a Quaker burial ground. Bear half right across the field to a wooden stile at the bottom leading to the lane to Spigot House. Turn left along the lane and cross a stone stile on the right in front of the house. Go down the field along the wall on the left to a gap stile followed very quickly by another. Now go across the slope to a third stile, in the corner, and follow the old wall on the right to reach the drive to Shepherd's Yeat. Continue along the drive to a narrow road.

The road leads left to the B5284 near Crook church, and could be a short cut in case of bad weather. Follow it in any case as far as Brow Head, the next farm, where the walk continues through the signposted gateway on the right, just before the farm buildings. (For a shorter and less strenuous route from Brow Head, turn right up the metalled road opposite the farmhouse – point A on the map – and rejoin the main route at point B.)

To continue the main route from Brow Head, beyond the gate head across the field and uphill to a wooden hand gate, and follow the waymarks half right to a stone stile. Continue steeply uphill to another stone stile in front of a clump of trees, from where there is a fine panoramic view of the South Lakeland fells. Now follow the wall on the left to reach High House Farm by a gate into the farmyard. Turn right to go round the end of the barn and over two stiles in succession immediately behind it. Continue over the top of the hill ahead. On the right is the Gilpin Valley, visited on Walk No. 7. Descend through a hand gate to reach the drive to Birk Moss, and follow it left, through a gate, and on round a double bend to reach the bottom of the drive to High House Farm (point B on the map). Turn right into the field.

Follow the wall on the left, ignoring a signpost to the right, to reach a gate at the bottom of the field, then keep straight ahead to join a raised track going along beside the hedge on the left. On reaching a gateway (with Crook Hall Farm away to the right), do not go through, but turn left, beside the wall, to a gap stile in the corner. Then bear right to visit the ruined tower of the former manor chapel, which ceased to be used over 100 years ago when Crook church was built. Crook Hall Farm was the site of the manorial hall in mediaeval times.

Beyond the chapel enclosure, aim towards Crook church, then follow the wall to the right to join a track going down to the main road and the start of the walk.

Walk No. 3

CUNSWICK SCAR   8km (5 miles)

You can easily complete this walk from Kendal in 2½ hours. It makes a pleasant evening stroll for anyone staying overnight in the town, with the possibility of supper from the takeaway shop on Hallgarth estate near the end of the walk. You can park in Queen's Road, near the beginning of the walk, but to avoid confusion follow the footpath sign opposite the north end of Low Fellside, not the one higher up Queen's Road near Serpentine Woods, pointing to Helsfell Nab.

Leave the centre of Kendal by Allhallows Lane opposite the town hall, and follow the first road on the right, Low Fellside, to its junction with Queen's Road. Now take the lane just across Queen's Road and follow the clearly-defined path across three fields and left of some allotments to reach a stile on the left of a ruined barn. Another stile ahead leads to another field. Climb gently with the wall on the right, across the next two fields via a kissing gate. Then cross the stile in the far corner of the

second field, next to a gate, to reach a path going along the bottom of a
steep wooded bank, Helsfell Nab. Continue to a gate, and across the next
field to a stile to the right of a barn. Turn left up the hill to the wall at the
top, and follow the wall left, above the trees, to the first of three large
wooden stiles leading to a footbridge over the bypass.

Continue beyond the bridge by taking the stile on the right, where a
distinct path crosses the open pasture, going left of an old rifle range. Go

Walk 3

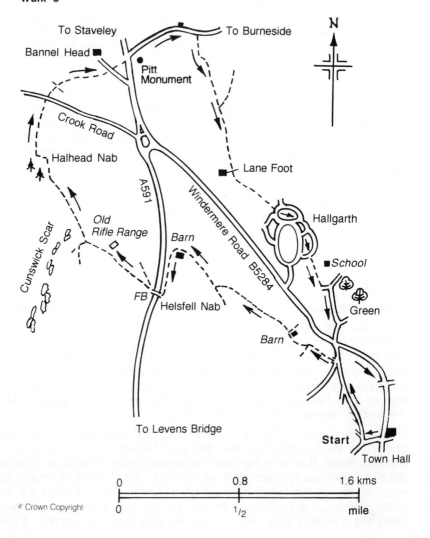

To Staveley

Bannel Head

To Burneside

N

Pitt
Monument

Crook Road

Halhead Nab

Lane Foot

A591

Hallgarth

Windermere Road B5284

Cunswick Scar

Old
Rifle Range

Barn

School

FB

Helsfell Nab

Green

Barn

To Levens Bridge

Start

Town Hall

© Crown Copyright

0   0.8   1.6 kms

0   1/2   mile

12

over the stile in the far corner onto the open fell, and make for the highest point, the cairn near Hallhead Nab. This is the northern extremity of the four-mile limestone escarpment that runs north and south on the west side of Kendal; it is a fine viewpoint for the fells of central Lakeland and the High Street area.

On leaving the summit continue forward, bearing slightly left to the edge of the scarp and a stile at the junction of a fence with a wall. Over the stile, follow the fence on the left over two more stiles, and bear right down the scarp and through the trees to reach a stile into a field. Cross the field to the main Kendal-Crook road, and go over the stile opposite. Continue beside the hedge on the left to another stile by a gate, and then keep the hedge on the right until it turns away at a right angle. Now bear half-left, aiming towards an obelisk-like monument to find two kissing gates crossing the drive to Bannel Head. Beyond the drive, cross the field diagonally to a wooden kissing gate and the busy A591 to Windermere.

Cross the main road with great care to the lane opposite, passing the monument to William Pitt on the right. After about 400m, and 120m after passing Eller Green Lodge on the left, cross a stone stile in a wall corner on the right. Follow the wall on the left for a bare 100m to a wall stile into the adjoining field. Then cross the corner of this field to a gap stile. Continue in the same direction to a wall stile, where a hedge abuts the wall opposite. Go straight ahead across the next field, passing between two low hills, to a curious iron ladder stile partly concealed in the hedge.

Cross the next field, aiming ahead for the buildings of Lane Foot farm (not the small house on the right) to find another wall stile in the corner of the field. Continue towards the farm, but do not go right up to the farmyard; instead go straight ahead to the field gate at the bottom of the farmhouse garden, and cross the corner of the next field to another gate. Now aim diagonally across the bottom of the next field to a stile in the far left corner, leading into a narrow path between two gardens.

Keep straight ahead to reach the main estate road, Hallgarth Circle, and follow it left, past the telephone kiosk and the takeaway shop. About 150m past the shops, opposite some open ground, turn left into Low Garth and very soon look for a tarmac path on the right, between the houses, heading for the primary school. Follow the path up the field and through a stile, and then bear left to reach Kendal Green. Turn right along the side of the green to reach Windermere Road via Green Road. Here turn left for the town centre, or continue across into Queen's Road.

Walk No. 4

THE WATCHGATE MORAINE   8.8km (5½ miles)

This is a gently undulating walk from Otter Bank on the A6. It is a ramble mainly over pasture land on the Watchgate moraine between the Kent, Sprint, and Mint valleys. The moraine consists of boulders, stones, and grit deposited by a retreating glacier at the end of the last ice age.

There is a large layby on the east side of the A6, about 5¼ km north of Kendal at the signpost to Whinfell. Take the minor road uphill for about 150m and then fork left up a partially metalled lane, which rises over the moraine. After about 1km you reach another road; turn left here, and after a few metres go through a field gate on the right. A grassy cart track meanders pleasantly across two large fields and one small one, then reaches a gate into a narrow lane leading to Selside school. Go past the school buildings to the road.

Continue along the road to the next junction, go through a field gate on the right, labelled "Steel Croft", and follow the track across the field. After going through a wall opening, leave the track and go through a gate on the right and straight across the field to another gate, which leads to a cart track that bears left over the shoulder of the hill. Follow this track, which goes below a clump of trees to Bouthwaite farm. Go straight through the farmyard and out through three consecutive gates leading to a pylon. Beyond the pylon, follow the wall up to the gate on the right at the top of the field (not the facing gate), and after going through the gate turn left and continue with the wall on your left. Half way down the slope to the road, bear right to the junction of a wall and hedge, where a stone step stile leads onto the road.

Turn right along the road for 120m, go through the first gateway on the left, and head towards a pylon. Across the field, a good footbridge over the Light Water takes the right of way to the right of the house at Whitwell Folds and onto its drive; bear left through the yard. Continue through a waymarked gate beyond the yard and across the field to another gate, ignoring the first gate, which leads into the field on the right. Keep following the hedge/wall on the right to the bottom of the next field. There are impressive views of the Howgill Fells ahead, and Whinfell Beacon (with its prominent cairn) half left. Go through the gateway ahead and, turning sharp right, follow up the hedge to a stone stile; then go straight across another field to a gateway. A few metres beyond this gate, bear left to contour along the bottom of the field and reach the bank of the River Mint. Continue to a stile in the corner of the field, beyond which is a small footbridge over the old mill leat, now no more than a weedchoked ditch at this point. Keep going right, beside the leat, to a stile with a lifting bar. Continue alongside the attractive rapids of the Mint to reach the road

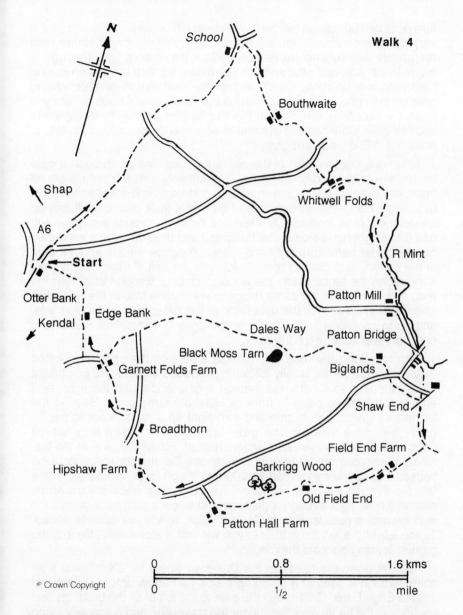

Walk 4

School

Bouthwaite

Shap

A6

Whitwell Folds

R Mint

Start

Otter Bank

Patton Mill

Edge Bank

Kendal

Dales Way

Patton Bridge

Black Moss Tarn

Garnett Folds Farm

Biglands

Shaw End

Broadthorn

Field End Farm

Hipshaw Farm

Barkrigg Wood

Old Field End

Patton Hall Farm

0   0.8   1.6 kms

0   1/2   mile

by a narrow gateway at Patton Mill, believed to be of mediaeval origin. Follow the river to Patton Bridge.

At the bridge, bear right for a few metres, then go left up a lane in front of two cottages and a telephone box. Continue for 200m, passing under an archway which carries the drive to Shaw End. Beyond the archway turn right for 100m to an old barn, then bear left between walls and past a very old drinking trough. You are now on the Dalesway long-distance path for about 300m, and there are yellow waymarks. Go through a waymarked gate, and after another 100m bear left through an iron kissing gate onto a good drive. Continue over the next rise to another kissing gate on the right, just beyond a clump of mature beech trees, where you leave the Dalesway. Go through the kissing gate and up by the fence to another gate. Continue in the same direction, with the wall on the left, to reach Field End via a field gate.

Turn right, pass in front of the old farmhouse, and go through a gate beside the cattle grid to the drive. Immediately turn left onto a gravel track, which goes past a converted barn and leads into a walled lane. On reaching a field, keep straight ahead on a faint track over the hill, beside an electricity pole, to reach Old Field End farm. Go through two gates and round the right-hand side of the buildings, and drop down to a wide gate beside the far barn. Turn right and cross the narrow field to another gate at the bottom, and climb diagonally towards the belt of trees on the right. Keep along the fence below the wood to cross a wooden stile near the end, and continue in the same direction via a stone stile in the wall. Now follow a diverted path to the right-hand of two gates across the next field, and on to another gate leading onto the drive to Patton Hall Farm. Turn right up the drive to reach the road.

Turn left along the road for 150m to a stile on the right, signposted "Hipshow Farm". After initially following the hedge on the right, go straight across the field to a barn. Go through a gate and round the right-hand end of the barn to pass in front of Hipshow farmhouse. Beyond the farmhouse go through a gate and turn right up a rough track to the far gate, beside a stream; the gate leads into a green lane which unfortunately also serves as a water channel. Follow the lane to the top, where it emerges onto a road at Broadthorn. Go straight ahead past the houses and up the minor road for 200m to a sign to Garnett Folds on the left. Go through the gate and follow the old sunken track ahead. At the next wall bear right through a gateway and follow a faint track across the field towards a gate leading to Garnett Folds, which you can see ahead. To the left of the left-hand house, you will find a stone wall stile into the garden, leading out onto the road.

Turn left down the road (on the Dalesway again for 200m), and after going through a gate, turn sharp right along a narrow unfenced metalled road to Edge Bank. Go through the gate to the left of all the buildings and continue in the same direction, under the power line and diagonally along the field, to a fancy iron handgate, and beyond it, across the corner of the next field, another gate. Contour around the edges of the next two fields, keeping above the boundaries on the left, to emerge onto the road via a stile at the starting point of the walk.

Walk No. 5

HAVERBRACK BANK AND THE FAIRY STEPS 8.8km (5½ miles)

The estate of Dallam Tower, through which this walk passes, comprises large tracts of natural woodland on limestone pavements. The estate is managed for shooting, and you will see a lot of pheasants; please keep dogs on a lead at all times. The trees are a riot of colour in autumn.

For those dependent on public transport, it is an easy walk of about 800m from the traffic lights at Milnthorpe to the nearest point of the walk. Go along Park Road, the Arnside road, until you reach a footbridge on the left over the River Bela, at the end of the built-up area. Cross the bridge into Dallam Park and bear right along the river bank to reach a gate onto the road in front of Dallam Tower House. This brings you onto the route of the walk. Turn right to complete the last section of the walk first.

If you are travelling by car, to avoid parking charges in Milnthorpe park by the entrance to the quarry on the Arnside road, about 1½ km west of the traffic lights at Milnthorpe (GR 483812). Quarry vehicles have a large turning circle, so leave plenty of room.

Look for a gap in the wire fence on the left of the entrance drive and follow the left-hand signpost along the bottom of the wood to a ladder stile into a field. Keep beside the wall on the left to another stile and cross a cart track to a third, leading into another wood. Fork right inside the wood and follow the path gently uphill, to go alongside a wall around the edge of the wood and emerge onto a lane at a stile.

Cross the narrow road to a kissing gate and climb beside the wall on the left, with fine views behind, across the Kent estuary. Go through another kissing gate at the top of the field, about 30m from the corner. Follow the sign pointing to Cockshot Lane, to reach a good broad track descending gently through open woodland, and later going into a denser wood. On approaching a wall you will find another signpost, which marks the beginning of some tricky navigation as there are many unofficial paths.

Turn right at the signpost, towards Sandside. If you want to play safe, bear left at the next junction and follow the path down to the road. Don't cross the stile onto the road, but follow the right-of-way sign sharp right, towards Sandside. However, this is going round two sides of a triangle, and the more adventurous can take a short cut. After turning right at the first signpost bear right at the first fork, near an old rusty iron post, then straight across at the next cross paths (by another iron post) and continue on in this direction, gently descending until reaching a T-junction in front of some crags. Turn left here and follow the path, with the crags on the right, until you join the main right-of-way coming from the road. (See the sketch map.) Turn right along this main path, which goes approximately

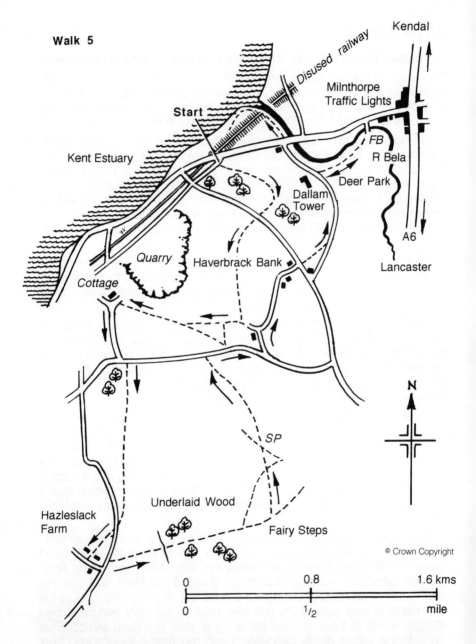

Walk 5

Kendal

Disused railway

Milnthorpe
Traffic Lights

Start

Kent Estuary

FB

R Bela

Deer Park

Dallam
Tower

A6

Lancaster

Quarry

Haverbrack Bank

Cottage

N

SP

Underlaid Wood

Hazleslack
Farm

Fairy Steps

© Crown Copyright

0   0.8   1.6 kms

0   ½   mile

north-west and gradually improves, running downhill beside crags on the
left, until reaching a stile in the corner of a field. Keep along the edge of
the field to another stile opposite a cottage.

Turn left in front of the cottage, then left again at the next junction, signposted "Beetham". Continue on the road for about 400m, noting the yew trees clinging precariously to the rocks on the right, to reach another T-junction. Turn left and look for a footpath sign to Hazelslack about 100m on the right.

Keep along beside the wall on the right across the next two fields, going through a short length of walled lane in a wood between the two. Towards the end of the third field go over a stile on the right to reach the road by a field gate. Cross the road to another stile and aim across the field for Hazelslack farm, with its interesting 14th-century pele tower.

Enter the farm precincts by a stile close to the house (empty at the time of writing) and follow the drive to the road. Turn left to reach a T-junction with the road previously crossed.

Keep straight ahead to the stile opposite, signposted to the Fairy Steps. This is part of the Limestone Link, a medium-distance path between Arnside and Kirkby Lonsdale, but despite the blue arrows not a bridleway at this point. Follow the track across two fields and into Underlaid Wood, where it rises gently over the limestone pavement. Before long the track begins to rise more steeply, and zig-zags up some narrow steps between the two rock faces. This is the route along which coffins had to be brought for burial at Beetham church in years gone by when there was no church at Arnside. The steps are not the Fairy Steps, however.

Continue upwards until you reach quite a high rock face with many clefts. Here, in a very narrow crevice, you will find the Fairy Steps. Indeed, you do need a rather fairylike figure to negotiate the steps with any comfort. (Should they prove impassable, take the path that leads left from the bottom of the steps to the signpost mentioned further on.) On reaching the top of the steps, having paused to admire the view over the estuary (seen best when the leaves are off the tress), leave the blue arrows and turn left along the edge of the escarpment. Soon after the path becomes rough over the limestone "clints" and "grikes", it descends left over the rocks to join another broad grassy track going north-west across open ground towards a signpost. Keep straight on past the signpost, following the smooth path as it descends through woodland for about 800m to reach a road.

Turn right along the road for about 300m, ignoring a signpost on the left into the wood, and turn left at the end of the wood onto a dirt road, signposted "Haverbrack". At the next junction bear right, following the Haverbrack sign again, and, passing the two or three houses that constitute the hamlet of Haverbrack, emerge onto a narrow metalled lane. (A left turn here gives a short cut back to the first road crossing and the parked car.) To complete the walk, go through the stile across the lane into Dallam Park and, keeping in the same direction, go downhill to a kissing gate onto the public road through the park. Turn left along the road, looking out for deer in the park on the right, and follow it past Dallam Tower House to join the main Arnside road near Milnthorpe Bridge over the River Bela.

Cross the road to the stile opposite and follow the river bank past the weir and along to its junction with the Kent estuary. Whitbarrow Scar is straight ahead. Continue round by the estuary shore until you come to a narrow, raking path leading onto the remains of the old railway line, which used to link Arnside with the main line near Hincaster. Follow the old track back to the Arnside road, emerging by the quarry entrance and the parked car.

Walk No. 6

HELSINGTON BARROWS AND SCOUT SCAR   8.8km (5¼ miles)

This walk visits one of the favourite haunts of the people of Kendal, who, though spoilt for choice with so much lovely country around, return again and again to Scout Scar for a Sunday afternoon or evening stroll. Helsington Barrows is a beautiful stretch of National Trust open woodland.

There are several routes up to the Scar, but this is perhaps the least used. The walk starts from the south end of Kendal on the A6 (Milnthorpe Road), and follows a very straight line across fields of pasture, hay, or silage, according to season. Please keep in single file when the grass is long, but don't go round the edges of the fields. You can leave a car on the verge near the filling station at the edge of the built-up area (beside the parish boundary stone), where the walk finishes. The nearest bus stop is Lumley Road.

Go up the signposted drive on the opposite (west) side of the A6, and after 150m turn left at the junction in front of Helsington Laithes. Follow this drive for 300m and, immediately after passing under the bypass by a high tunnel (in which you can hear wonderful echoes), go through a field gate on the left. Follow the fenced cart track to the next gate, and then bear half left across the field to another gate with a very narrow squeeze stile beside it. Continue in the same direction diagonally across the corner of this field to a stile left of a solitary ash tree.

Keep going in the same direction, diagonally across the fields, using first a gate left of an old stone stile that you can still see buried in the hedge, and then the left-hand one of two gates across the next field. After the following field, you have to negotiate the end of a very muddy fenced cart track to reach a gate into the corner of the last field before High House farm. Now aim well left of the buildings to find a gap stile in the next wall. Continue along the next field parallel to the wall on the right, passing an old lime kiln, to reach a narrow road via another stone wall stile.

Walk 6

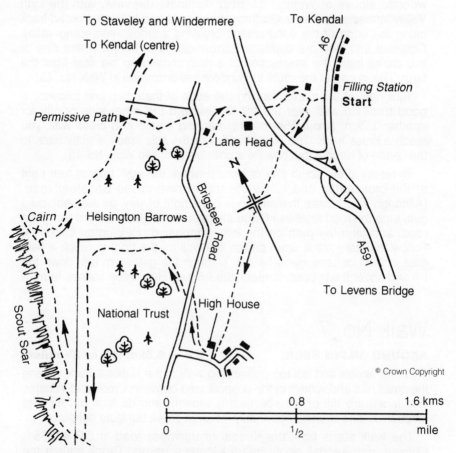

To Staveley and Windermere

To Kendal (centre)

To Kendal

A6

Filling Station
Start

Permissive Path

Lane Head

N

Brigsteer Road

Cairn

Helsington Barrows

A591

To Levens Bridge

Scout Scar

National Trust

High House

© Crown Copyright

| 0 | | 0.8 | | 1.6 kms |

0   ½   mile

Turn right up the road and, 75m past the entrance to High House farm on the right, cross a wall stile on the right. This cuts off a corner by following a faint track along the field and into its narrow neck, to emerge onto the Brigsteer road via a stile next to a gate at its far end.

Turn left up the road for about 50m to a gate on the right leading into the National Trust access land. Now follow the broad track ahead, continuing as it bears left alongside a wall. At the summit of the hill in the angle of the wall, a small cairn marks a magnificent view in all directions: from Morecambe Bay, to the Lakeland fells, Whinfell Beacon, and the Howgill Fells; and you can even see the summit of Ingleborough through the trees, peeping over the Leck fells.

Turn left with the wall and continue along the track that descends beside the wall, ignoring any forks to the left, until you reach a gate in the

21

wall leading out of the National Trust property. On the descent, the wooded slopes of Whitbarrow Scar dominate the view, with the Lyth Valley immediately below. Go through the gate and follow the broad track along the edge of the escarpment, crossing a small intersecting valley. Continue until you are opposite Barrowfield farm, below, where one or two cairns mark the intersection of a path coming up the scar from the farm. This is part of the route to Windermere described in Walk No. 15.

Turn right at the cairns, leaving the edge of the scarp and following a good track up and over the hill to descend the other side gently for another 1.2km. About 75m before reaching a stile in a cross wall, you reach a cross track. The way ahead over the stile leads directly back to the centre of Kendal (but beware a possible bull: see Walk No. 15).

To return to the south end of Kendal where the walk began, turn right at the crosspaths and follow the track down to the Brigsteer road. (Although much used, this stretch is not a right of way, as the padlocked gate onto the road testifies.) Climb the gate, turn right, go 200m along the road, and take the path on the left (signposted "Helsington Laithes"). Follow the stony track down beside the wall on the right to reach a field gate in front of Lane Head house. Through the gate, turn left, down the hill and under the bypass, to reach the A6 past Helsington Laithes farm.

Walk No. 7

AROUND GILPIN BECK   8.8 or 5.5km (5½ or 3½ miles)

This is a flexible and not too demanding walk in the National Park, among the small hills and valleys of the unspoilt area between Crook and Winster. The lanes are full of blackberries in season, and do look out for wild raspberries and strawberries in July – they're small, but taste delicious.

The walk starts from the Kendal to Bowness road at GR 438951. Coming from Kendal, about half a kilometre beyond Crook church the road passes a farm on the left with a letter box near the gate. Before the road descends fairly steeply and swings to the right in front of some white cottages, there is a rough layby on the left opposite two bungalows, with room for several cars.

Go down an unsigned path to the left of the white cottages and turn left on reaching a lane. About 150m along the lane is Spigot House, and in the wall opposite the south side of the house is a stile by a gate into a field. Over the stile bear half right, diagonally down the field to a gate at the bottom, and follow the hedge down the next field to where you will find a stile and a small clapper bridge. Turn right beyond the bridge and follow the broken wall on the left to a larger clapper bridge, over the Gilpin Beck.

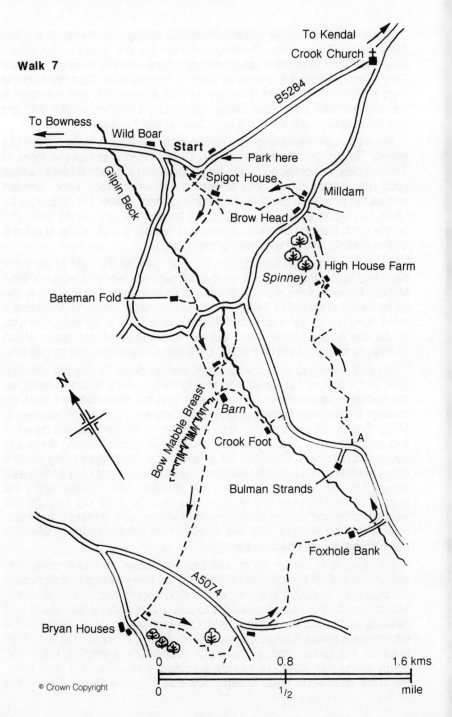

Walk 7

To Kendal

Crook Church

To Bowness

Wild Boar

Start

B5284

Park here

Spigot House

Milldam

Gilpin Beck

Brow Head

High House Farm

Spinney

Bateman Fold

Bow Mabble Breast

Barn

Crook Foot

A

Bulman Strands

Foxhole Bank

A5074

Bryan Houses

N

© Crown Copyright

0   0.8   1.6 kms

0   1/2   mile

Continue to the corner of the field and go through the middle one of the three gates. Then follow the fence/wall on the left, going south, which eventually lead to a green lane, and from there into the drive to Bateman Fold. Continue down the drive to reach a narrow road. Turn right up the road for 200m and, where it swings right up a steep hill, turn left down a partially-metalled lane. After about 400m pass a junction on the left, and you will shortly reach a fine old bank barn straight ahead.

Here you can take a short cut, reducing the walk to a mere 5.5 km (3½ miles). To do this, turn left in front of the barn and right in front of Thornyfields, the cottages on the left, to go down a good bridleway, which soon runs beside Gilpin Beck towards the drive of Crook Foot. Turn left across the bridge on the drive to reach the road. Follow the road right for 500m (¼ mile) to a gate on the left (50m beyond the drive to the next farm on the right, Bulman Strands), where you rejoin the main route at point A on the map. Omit the next three paragraphs.

To complete the full walk, go through the gate on the right of the bank barn and follow the cart track up the hill, with the wooded crags of Bow Mabble Breast on the right. The route is easy to follow, continuing in the same direction for about a kilometre, and eventually dropping down to the main Winster Valley road (A5074). This is a fairly busy road, but you could use it as another short cut by following it left for about 450m (¼ mile) to the next lane on the left. Omit the next paragraph if you do this.

Cross the main road to another gate and go down beside the wall to a gate in the bottom corner leading to a bridleway. After 400m (¼ mile), as the bridleway approaches some houses and the next metalled road, go through a gate, and follow the sign to the left, which points to Hawkearth Moss. Follow the cart track for another 400m, to where it passes between two concrete posts near a yew tree and piles of rubble marking the site of some old buildings. Continue for a few metres before heading off left, down the steep hill, through bracken. The old track is not easy to see as it swings left and then aims towards the wooden gate halfway along the stretch of woodland at the far side of a marshy field. Go through the wooden gate and up the field, over very wet ground, to find a gate and stile at the top leading onto the A5074. Turn left for 120m to where a narrow lane doubles back to the right.

Go along the lane for 300m past two bungalows, to find a stone step stile in the wall on the left, near the end of the trees (opposite a signpost). Go diagonally across the corner of the rough open land to a ladder stile, and continue in the same direction to join a cart track, which leads to a gateway and on across the next field. On reaching a gate at the top of the hill, the track disappears in a pasture field. After a descent of about 150m towards the Gilpin Valley, the track reappears, swinging right and going along the contours beside a ruined wall. After the next gate, the track descends quite steeply towards Foxhole Bank. Follow the well-waymarked route around the left of the buildings to reach the drive across a field, and continue along the drive, over Gilpin Beck to the road. Turn left along the road for 400m (¼ mile) to find a signposted gate on the right, just 50m before the entrance to Bulman Strands farm.

Go through the gate and aim half left up the hill, crossing one small tributary and keeping above the main beck, to reach a gate. Continue up the hill and, after passing the crags on the right, go through a gap in the old hedge and straight up the field to a gate, and follow the short green lane left to its end. The track now runs up the wall to the right, and then bears left between the outcrops, aiming for the tall trees ahead. Go through the gateway to the right of the trees, where fine views of the Lakeland fells open up; behind, on a clear day, between the hills there is a glimpse of Morecambe Bay, with Heysham power station beyond. Keep following the track, and on reaching the next gate keep straight ahead along the wall on the left to reach High House farm.

Bear left in the farmyard, in front of the barn, then left again in front of the house. Go past the wood heap and a stone-built chicken house on the left to reach a gate in the corner. Follow the wall on the right over the hill to reach a step stile in the corner of the field. Then aim diagonally down the slope to another step stile beside an ash tree, and on to a hand gate across the next field. Aim for the farm ahead, Brow Head, emerging onto the road at a field gate left of the buildings. Turn right, past the farm and down the hill for 120m, to Milldam. Turn left down a cart track between the beck and the barn, and follow the track all the way back to Spigot House and the start of the walk.

Walk No. 8

SIZERGH CASTLE OR BRIGSTEER 8.8 or 10.4km (5½ or 6½ miles) WOODS AND THE RIVER KENT

There is a choice on this walk of visiting either of two National Trust properties. The first is Sizergh Castle, the home of the Hornyold-Stricklands, which dates from 1340 AD, but is mainly Elizabethan. The house has beautiful grounds, including a remarkable rock garden. It is open Sunday to Thursday from 1.30 p.m. (grounds from 12.30 p.m.). The alternative route visits Brigsteer Woods, which are famous for their wild flowers, especially the daffodils, which lie dormant under the trees but in March spring up in profusion in those parts of the woods that have been felled. Information boards explain how the woods are being managed for the maximum benefit to wildlife.

Leave the car at Force Bridge (GR 507868), which you reach by following the Sedgwick road for 400m (¼ mile) from the roundabout at the junction of the A590 and A591, 4 miles south of Kendal. Bus travellers can start the walk at the bus stop on the A590 immediately south of this roundabout.

Follow the footpath sign marked "Fell Side" on the west side of the bridge and, after crossing the dual carriageway with great care, go down the Barrow slip road and bear left around the roundabout. Now cross the

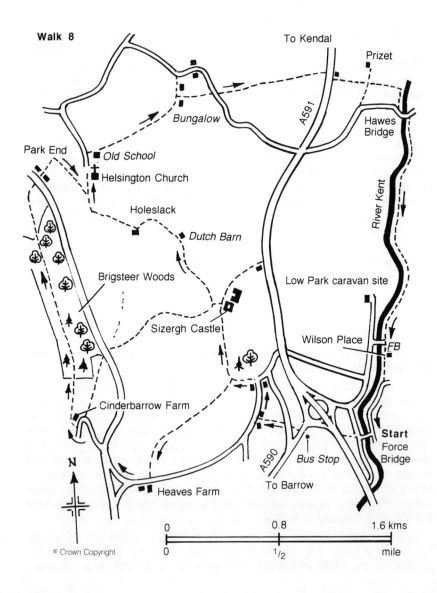

Walk 8

To Kendal

Prizet

Bungalow

A591

Hawes Bridge

Park End

Old School

Helsington Church

River Kent

Holeslack

Dutch Barn

Brigsteer Woods

Low Park caravan site

Sizergh Castle

Wilson Place

FB

Cinderbarrow Farm

Start
Force Bridge

N

A590

Bus Stop

To Barrow

Heaves Farm

© Crown Copyright

0		0.8		1.6 kms
0		1/2		mile

26

main Barrow road (A590) to a bus stop, where steps lead up the embankment to a footpath sign and stile a few metres to the left. Go straight across the field to a wall stile and cross the road into a green lane. Where the lane emerges via the drive of Fell Side farm onto another road, turn right for about 300m to a terrace of cottages on the left. Go up the track in front of the cottages, bearing left to a gate and a stile. Immediately after the stile, leave the track and cross two stiles close to the wall on the right. Continue up the hill, close to the wall, until you reach two gates at the end of the wood. Here the routes divide. To take the longer route, via Brigsteer Woods, omit the next two paragraphs.

To reach Sizergh Castle, cross the stile on the left of the two gates and follow the wall on the right along the field to emerge in the visitors' car park at the castle. Continue along the length of the car park to reach a narrow opening in the wall giving access to the castle shop and the ticket office.

After a possible visit to the house and grounds, continue the walk by going a few metres up the green lane opposite the stable yard, to where a gate on the right leads into a field. Cross the field to a gate opposite and continue along the cart track to a Dutch barn. Keep on this track, bearing left past the old farmhouse of Holeslack, up the hill and along the escarpment, until you reach Helsington church. Omit the next three paragraphs.

To follow the route via Brigsteer Woods, go half left, diagonally across the field ahead, aiming left of the high ground, to the top left corner of the field, and go through a gap in the old hedge near its junction with a transverse wall. As you reach the crest of the hill, fine views open up of Whitbarrow Scar, its wooded slopes fringing the Lyth Valley. Continue in the same direction, downhill, aiming towards Whitbarrow Scar, and near the bottom corner of the wood on the left go through a small wicket gate. Now bear left along the cart track to reach a road via a stile 20m to the right of the gate, opposite Heaves Farm.

Turn right along the road, and right at the next junction. At the crossroads go straight across and down the hill, with distant views of the Lakeland fells. Levens village is spread along the hillside behind, and Burnbarrow Scar is over on the right. The footpath sign on the right at the sharp left-hand bend in the road points the way to the upper part of Brigsteer woods, where car-borne visitors park. This may be the best way to take at daffodil time, as the daffodils seem more abundant in the upper part of the woods; you can rejoin the main route by following one of the slanting tracks that descend to the right of way at the bottom of the woods. At other times continue down the lane and, just past all the buildings of Cinderbarrow farm, go down a farm track on the right, and follow it below the farm buildings. Where the track swings left onto the "moss", go straight ahead into the wood.

Sizergh Castle

Continue along the level track the full length of the woods to reach a field at the north end. Now go half right across the middle of the field towards the farm ahead, Park End, reaching the road via a gate in the corner of the field. Turn left along the road as far as the farmhouse, and go up the forecourt in front of the house to a small wicket gate over a stream. (This is the true right of way, but the farmer permits the use of the gates beside the barn, opposite the point of access to the road.) Head up the steep field to the top left corner, where a gate gives access to a stony track that continues upwards to reach the open hillside. Helsington church is close to the tall trees that you can see on the skyline, but the path follows an easier gradient up the raking track to the right. Where this track reaches the farm road along the escarpment, double back left towards the church.

St John's church, Helsington, formerly a daughter church of Kendal, was built in 1726, and endowed by John Jackson of Holeslack Farm. It is well worth a visit for the interesting mural depicting local scenery, and the unique tooled-leather altar panels.

Both routes now go up the wall beside the old school buildings, north of the church. Keeping close to the wall on the right, follow the rough track over the top of the hill, where fine views unfold of the Howgill Fells, near Sedbergh, in the distance, and Whinfell Beacon half left. Continue until the track reaches a bungalow on the right. Just past the bungalow, at the end of a high stone wall, turn right through a field gate and go down the side of the garden, through a cypress hedge to another wide gate in the bottom right-hand corner, leading into a field. Bear left across the field, following a faint track to a gate at the bottom. Cross the lane to another gate and go straight across the middle of the next two fields to a stile on the left of the gate at the end of the second field. Now follow the fence or hedge on the left down, via stiles, to reach the main road.

Cross the A591 with great care and go up the drive beside the old lodge to Prizet House opposite, When you reach a tarmac drive at right angles, go straight across on a diverted path that crosses two stiles and descends beside the hedge on the left to reach the River Kent. Turn right along the river bank to reach Natland Lane and Hawes Bridge.

Cross the bridge to a stile into a field and turn right to follow the east bank of the Kent downstream to Force Bridge, where the walk began. You can cross to the west bank at Wilson Place footbridge, but in any case the last 500m is on metalled roads.

Walk No. 9

TWO MERES WALK   **12km (7½ miles)**

This is a good leg-stretching walk, some of it on roads, over generally windswept upland pastures above Old Town, near Kirkby Lonsdale. In part it uses the Scotch drove road, along which thousands of head of cattle were driven from Scottish pastures to northern markets. Choose a clear day to make the most of the stunning views towards the Middleton and Barbon fells. Old Town, where the walk starts, is three miles north west of Kirkby Lonsdale on the B6254 from Kendal, at GR 596830. Parking is limited to road verges, and it is hard to find one that has not been neatly mown in front of the houses. However, these verges are part of the highway and parking is perfectly legitimate.

From Old Town take the minor road north, the old Scotch road, signposted to Killington and Sedbergh. After climbing gently for about 1.2km (¾ mile), just past a gorse covered embankment on the right and towards the crest of the hill, go through a field gate on the left and follow a good hard track down beside a ruined wall. Follow this track for about 1.2km (¾ mile), passing over the Blea Beck outflow from Wyndhammere, one of our two tarns, at the bottom of the hill, to reach the B6254.

Turn right up the main road for another 1.2km, passing a lane on the right marked "Middle Fell House", and another on the left down which you can see Lupton reservoir and Tarnhouse Tarn. On reaching Barkin House, on the right among trees at the top of the hill (at the time of writing undergoing a barn conversion), pass the ends of two drives and a small wood to go through a field gate just beyond the wood. Follow the wall on the right beside the wood to enter the yard by the corner of a building. (You may prefer to go up the second drive.) Bear left past two stock sheds to leave the yard by the left- hand one of two gates, ignoring the grassy lane beyond the right-hand gate. On reaching a field, continue in the same direction beside the wall on the right to a gate in the far corner. Continue with the wall now on the left as it curves round to the left over the top of a hill with fine views and enters a green lane; Wyndhammere is below on the right.

At the end of the green lane go sharp right through a gate to follow the wall down to a stony track. Turn left along the track past the semi-derelict High Fell House, bearing slightly right to a gate beyond a large ash tree. Keep on the terraced grass track to the bottom of the hill, and then climb to a gate above the top corner of the plantation. Continue along the field above the plantation until, at its end, you join a cart track at right angles. Turn left along the cart track to reach the old Scotch drove road again.

Turn left along the road for 350m to a gate on the right signposted to Rigmaden. Follow this bridleway over the top of the hill, passing Kitmere Tarn, our second tarn, which is largely hidden among rhododendrons, on

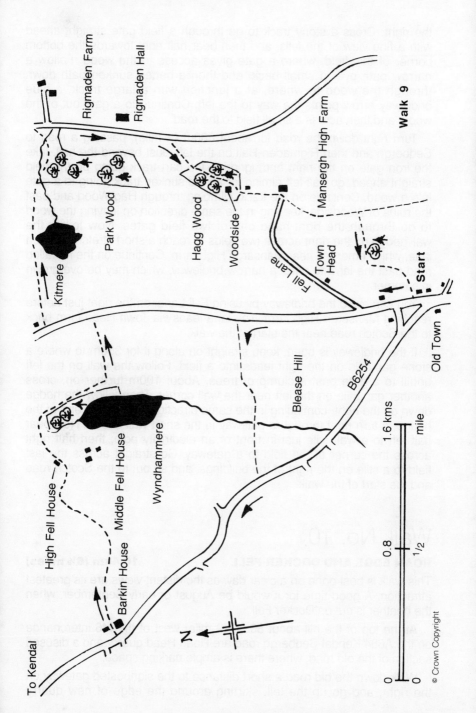

© Crown Copyright

the right. Cross a stony track to go through a field gate straight ahead with a fine view of the fells, and then bear half right towards the bottom corner of this field, where a gate gives access to the wood. Follow a narrow path over a small beck, and then a better, sunken path down through the wood to where, at a junction with a large track, a blue bridleway arrow points the way to the left. Continue to a gate out of the wood, and then across a small field to the road.

Turn right down the road for about 800m (½ mile), passing a road to Sedbergh and then Rigmaden Hall on the left. Just beyond the hall, take the iron gate on the right and, ignoring the cart track going up the field straight ahead, go half left aiming for an old sunken track going to a gate into a wood. Continue on the track, climbing through Hag Wood and past the ruins of Woodside, keeping in the same direction on leaving the wood to go through the right-hand one of two field gates. Now follow the wall/hedge on the right across two fields to reach a short stretch of green lane, which emerges near Mansergh High farm. Continue on the metalled road past the farm to enter a narrow bridleway, which may be overgrown in summer.

You can avoid the bridleway by using Fell Lane, on the right just before reaching Mansergh High farm. The lane leads via Town Head farm back to the Scotch road near the start of the walk.

If the bridleway is open, keep straight on along it for 350m to where a stone gap stile on the right leads into a field. Follow the wall on the left uphill to a gate past a clump of trees. About 100m further on, cross another gap stile on the left near the wall corner. Then follow the hedge down on the right, continuing in the same direction beyond the end of the hedge to turn right through a gateway in the short wall ahead. Now bear half left to a wall stile just in front of an electricity pole, then half right across the corner of the field to a gateway. Go straight across the last field to a stile on the right of the buildings, and so out to the Scotch road and the start of the walk.

Walk No. 10

ROAN EDGE AND DOCKER FELL　　　　　　10.4km (6½ miles)

This walk is best done on a clear day, as the distant views are its greatest attraction. A good time for it would be August or early September, when the heather is out on Docker Fell.

At the top of the hill about 800m (½ mile) west of the M6 interchange on the A684 Kendal-Sedbergh road are Roan Head quarry and a disused section of the old road, where there is ample parking space.

Walk down the old road a short distance to the signposted gateway on the right, and go up the fell, skirting around the edge of new quarry

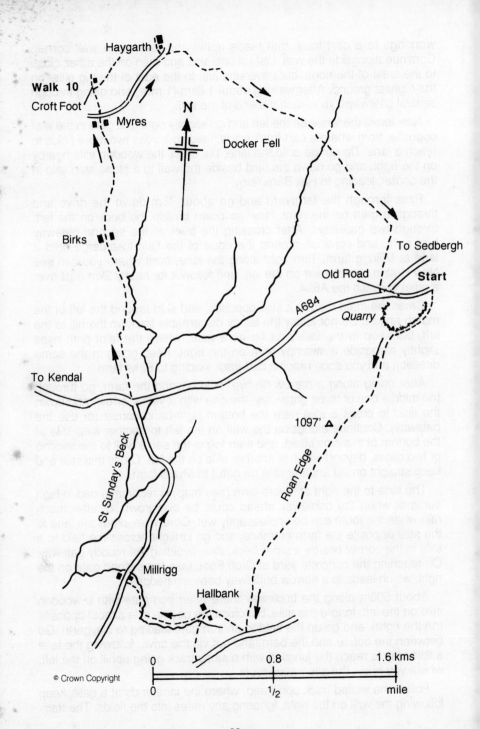

Haygarth

Walk 10

Croft Foot

Myres

Docker Fell

N

Birks

To Sedbergh

Old Road

Start

A684

Quarry

To Kendal

1097' △

St Sunday's Beck

Roan Edge

Millrigg

Hallbank

0   0.8   1.6 kms

© Crown Copyright

0   ½   mile

workings to a cart track that leads uphill and reaches a wall corner. Continue alongside the wall, first on one side and then on the other, close to the crest of the ridge, but traversing just to the east of the trig pillar on the highest ground. After walking about 1.6km (1 mile) and going through several gateways, you reach the end of the wall.

Now leave the fence on the left and go slightly right to a gate in the wall opposite, from where a cart track starts, leading across two more fields to reach a lane. Do not go onto the lane, but cross the wooden stile nearby on the right, and go down the field beside the wall to a stone step stile in the corner, leading to Hall Bank farm.

Pass through the farmyard and go about 75m down the drive and through a gate on the right. Now go down beside the beck on the left, through two gateways. After crossing the beck at the second gateway turn right, and continue around the edge of the field to emerge onto a lane at Millrigg farm. Turn right along the lane, from where you can see New Hutton church over on the left, and follow it for nearly 2km (just over a mile) to reach the A684.

Cross the main road to a stile opposite, and skirt around the left of the marsh ahead. Do not follow the faintly discernable track up the hill to the left, but keep in the valley as far as a gate, where the faint path rises slightly alongside a swampy area on the right. Keep going in the same direction and you soon reach a cart track leading to Birks farm.

After going along a narrow "in-bye" field beyond the farm, go through the middle one of three gateways (the one with a yellow arrow) and down the field to cross a stile near the bottom right-hand corner (or use the gateway). Continue alongside the wall on the left to another step stile at the bottom of this small field, and then follow the same wall to the second of two gates, beyond which is another stile on the left. Cross this stile and keep straight on via another stile (or gate) to Myers farm.

The lane to the right at Myers farm (see map) is recommended in high summer when the bridleway ahead could be overgrown, or after much rain when the route can be unpleasantly wet. Otherwise, cross the lane to the stile opposite the farm entrance, and go straight across the field to a stile in the corner beside a small beck, thus avoiding the muddy gateway. On reaching the concrete yard at Croft Foot, take the second gate on the right, which leads to a narrow bridleway between hedges.

About 500m along the bridleway there is an iron gate with a wooden stile on the left. Ignore this stile, but cross the double stile almost opposite (on the right), and go up the field to an iron gate leading to Haygarth. Go between the house and the barn, and out via the drive, following the lane a little way to reach the junction with a stony track going uphill on the left, where you rejoin the alternative route.

Follow the walled track uphill and, where the lane ends at a gate, keep following the wall on the right, ignoring any gates into the fields. The track rises through the sparse heather for 750m until it reaches a saddle between two low hills. Here it becomes very faint, but bear slightly right at a hardly visible fork (towards the distant trig pillar on Roan Head), and soon you will notice the old bridleway again, marked by old wooden posts. Follow the bridleway as it bears left again to go diagonally down the slope into the valley, but first note the raking path going diagonally up the hillside opposite, which you will use to leave the valley. Follow this path and, when it levels out, aim for the convergence of two walls ahead, where there is a gate. Through the gate a rough track beside the wall on the right leads back to the A684 and the parked car.

Walk No. 11

WHITBARROW   10.4km (6½ miles)

Whitbarrow Scar is the imposing limestone outcrop to the north of the A590 about 3km (2 miles) west of Levens Bridge.

The view from the open fell at the top of the scar at 215m (706 feet) must be one of the most extensive in South Lakeland. The greater part of the walk is through delightful mixed woodland, and the whole area is one of great interest to naturalists.

There is an infrequent bus service between Kendal and Grange-over-Sands that passes near the foot of the scar: alight at the Gilpin Bridge Inn and walk west to join the old road. Car users should take the first turning on the right after Gilpin Bridge, which leads onto the old road. Continue for 500m beyond the cattle grid to the next turn on the right and park at this junction.

Walk along the drive to Raven's Lodge and follow the bridleway sign to the right beyond the buildings and along the foot of the scar under the old quarry. Continue on the dirt road to Rawsons, a recently converted farmhouse, and turn left beyond the old barn to go along the front of the house. Keep straight ahead beyond the house into the wood on a narrow path. Follow the path as it climbs, zigzagging first right and then left to go alongside a wall. On reaching a crossways, turn right on the forestry road. After another 400m, just before the track opens out into a large turning area, take a smaller track on the left and follow this for about a mile through pleasant woodland, ignoring any side turnings, until you come to another forestry road at a T-junction.

Follow the yellow waymark to the left, forking right at the next junction. Soon the track starts to descend. When you reach the next fork, follow the arrow to the left, where you start a long, steady climb to the top of the scar. First you pass a minor track on the right near a small cairn, and then much further up you reach a T-junction. Turn right here, and shortly you will come to a stone stile in a wall, leading into the Hervey Nature

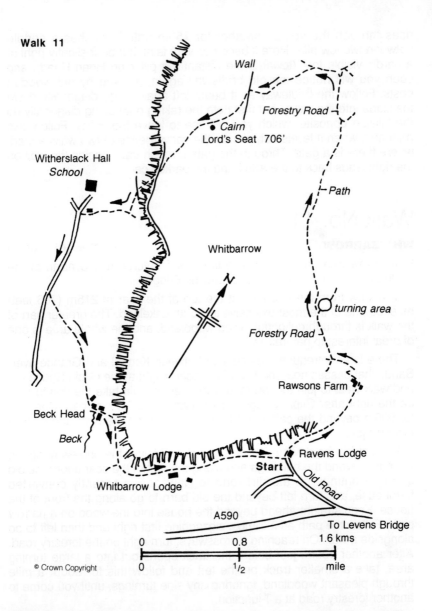

Wall

Forestry Road

● *Cairn*
Lord's Seat 706'

Witherslack Hall
School

Path

Whitbarrow

N

turning area

Forestry Road

Rawsons Farm

Beck Head

Beck

Ravens Lodge

Start

Old Road

Whitbarrow Lodge

A590

To Levens Bridge
1.6 kms

0   0.8

© Crown Copyright

0   ½   mile

Reserve. Over the wall, bear left along the path, which climbs to the highest point of the fell, marked by a monumental cairn with a plaque in memory of Canon Hervey, who founded the Lake District Naturalists' Trust.

The view from the top is a vast panorama, including the Coniston fells in the north west, and the High Street and Kentmere fells to the north, leading on to the Shap fells and Pennine moorlands. The Howgill Fells are to the north east, followed by Whernside and Ingleborough, with the Forest of Bowland to the south east across the Kent estuary. In the south is the vast expanse of Morecambe Bay from Heysham, with its two nuclear power stations, to Barrow-in-Furness. Arnside Knott and the railway viaduct are prominent in the middle distance.

From the summit, Lord's Seat, continue the walk in a westerly direction, towards another large cairn. Then follow the well-cairned path downwards to reach the edge of the scar, where it descends gradually along the edge beside a wall, and eventually crosses a stile into the wood below the wall. The descent from here through the wood is steep and tricky, especially after rain, but the path soon improves and levels out. Follow the signpost left at a fork, and you eventually go through a gap in the wall at the far side of the wood, leading to the football field of Witherslack Hall special school. Continue alongside the field to a stile, and then turn right on a grassy track that leads via a field gate to the road near the school entrance. Note the National Park's explanatory sign as you pass through the field gate.

Turn left along the road for 750m, and then follow the bridleway sign to the left. When you reach the hamlet of Beck Head keep on as far as the beck, which here emerges from the base of the limestone slabs like a miniature version of the River Aire at Malham Cove, no doubt giving the hamlet its name. After viewing this attractive feature, retrace your steps up the lane for about 50m to the right-hand one of two white field gates (with a footpath sign) just before reaching the stone cottage on the right.

Continue between the white houses, past a glasshouse on the left, to another signed gate leading into a field. Now follow the wall on the right to a stile into the wood, and continue on the track beside the wall until you emerge onto a stony drive. Turn left here and follow the drive up to Whitbarrow Lodge, where you pass all the buildings on your right by continuing up the grassy slope beyond the end of the drive. From here there is a pleasant path down through the wood to Raven's Lodge and back to the start of the walk.

Walk No. 12

KILLINGTON

12.8km (8 miles)

This lovely walk is mainly along the hillside overlooking the Lune valley. The first part is quite rugged, being partly over open moorland with tussock grass and no visible track, but you can avoid this by using the return route as far as Greenholme farm. The little hamlet of Killington is completely unspoilt despite its proximity to the motorway.

On the Kendal to Sedbergh road (A684), about 1.5km east of the motorway interchange, you come to a steep hill descending into the the Lune valley. A good half way down the hill on the left is a large layby near some trees, with an unsigned handgate opposite, where the walk starts. Unfortunately buses from Kendal to Sedbergh are few and far between.

Cross the road to the handgate and follow a faint old track going half right up the hill. Pass under the telephone wires and contour along beside them until you join a better grassy cart track. Bear left along this track to reach a gate. Through the gate, ignore the sign pointing right, along the fence, and go half left on another faint track towards the corner of a plantation.

Continue on a better track alongside the plantation, but where it forks at the end of the trees bear right, down into a broad valley. About 200m beyond the fork, you must leave the track as it heads towards more plantations, and bear left across the rough moorland, avoiding the bracken as far as possible, aiming to go around the left of the hill ahead near some old thorn trees. Here you can just detect the remains of an old track in the encroaching bracken. Follow this track around the base of the hill to reach a wall on the left, and follow the wall to a stile in the corner leading into an old green lane with ruined walls.

As the lane approaches Greenholme farm, go through a gate on the right above the paddock, leading to another gate into a large field. Contour along this field for 100m to a stile at the junction of a wall and hedge. Over the stile, continue along a cart track with the hedge on the right. Where the track goes through an opening in a wall, keep straight on to the derelict hedge ahead, and go through a gap near an old bathtub. Now gently descend the next field, aiming for the gate in the left-hand fence at the bottom. Through the gate, follow the fence on the right to another gate and then a gap stile, to drop down to the converted outbuildings of Killington Hall farm. Go over a wooden stile and a bridge into the garden of the first house, and down the drive to reach the old farmhouse and Killington church.

Killington Hall farm dates from the 15th century and was once the home of distinguished people, notably a speaker of the House of Commons. The church dates from the 14th century, but was restored in Victorian times.

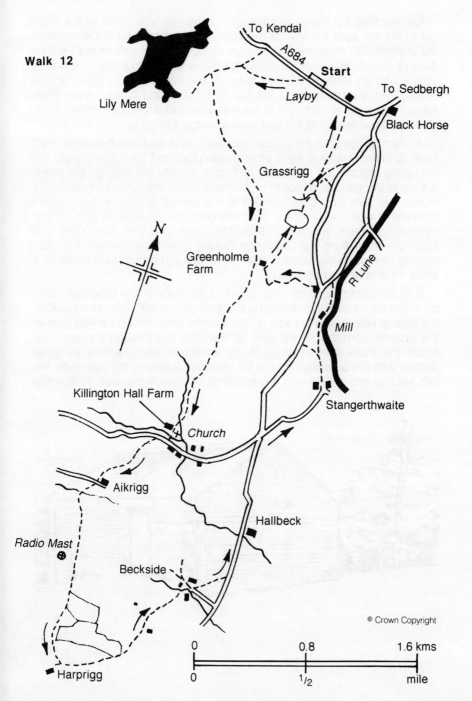

Walk 12

Lily Mere

To Kendal

A684

Start

Layby

To Sedbergh

Black Horse

Grassrigg

R Lune

Greenholme Farm

Mill

Stangerthwaite

Killington Hall Farm

Church

Aikrigg

Hallbeck

Radio Mast

Beckside

© Crown Copyright

Harprigg

0   0.8   1.6 kms

0   1/2   mile

N

On reaching the main road through the hamlet, you could take a short cut to the left, past the few houses and along the road for 800m to reach the crossroads* mentioned later, thus reducing the length of the walk by 3km (2 miles). However, to complete the walk turn right up the hill for 100m, and go through a small gate on the left with a footpath sign to Aikrigg. Go diagonally up to the top of the field and cross a stile. Then follow the hedge on the right to another stile, hidden in the corner of this field. Continue left along the cart track to reach Aikrigg farm via two gates.

At Aikrigg, go straight across the farm road and down another cart track to cross the beck by a small footbridge, and then go through the field gate beyond the ford. Now fork right, up the hill through the trees, aiming in the general direction of the radio mast. After reaching the crest of this rise, aim for a gate (derelict at the time of writing) in the junction between a wall and a fence. After climbing the gate, bear right to find another cart track, which climbs beside a wall to a field gate. (This is a slight deviation from the Ordnance Survey map, which shows the path leading to a now non-existent stile in the wall.) The field gate leads to a stony track near the radio mast.

Turn left along this track and, avoiding the track to the buildings, keep on in the same direction, following the wall on the left. After about 500m, the right of way leaves the wall on the left and goes through a field gate in the external corner of a wall over on the right. Go through the gate and follow the track as it crosses rough moorland and bracken, keeping parallel with the boundary on the left, to reach a gate in the corner on the left, leading into a field with the buildings of Harprigg ahead. Follow the

old sunken track around the edge of the field and, where it comes to a blocked opening in front of a stream (an old ford), go left around the bushes to join the track coming across the ford from Harprigg. Go left along this track towards a stone barn.

Passing to the right of the barn, the track descends gently alongside an old broken hedge on the right, continuing downwards through two gates and below the bottom of the wood. Keep going diagonally down the field below the wood, and cross another small field through two gates approximately halfway between a barn on the right and one over on the left. A third gate leads to an old sunken track alongside a hedge on the right. Follow this track down to another gate and out to a modern cart track, which leads down the field to Beckside. (The real right of way lies over the hedge on the left, but it is blocked and unusable; however, the farmer does not object to the use of the cart track.) Cross the bridge over the beck beyond the farmhouse, and a few metres along the farm access road to the right look for a narrow green lane on the left, which leads to the metalled road. Turn left and follow the road for about 1km to a crossroads*.

Turn right at the crossroads and go down a narrow lane leading to Stangerthwaite. Continue on the hard-surfaced road between the house and a fine three-storey barn. Where the lane bears left and uphill, keep straight ahead to a stile into a narrow green lane, which leads to the bank of the Lune. Follow the river bank to the old mill, which has now been converted into a house. The right of way continues through the buildings, but can be side-tracked by going round by the road (see map). However, it is an interesting part of the walk and worth the extra 400m (¼ mile) to continue on the waymarked route through a closed passage to the left of the mill house to look at the weir and millrace. Continue along the river bank, over a stile and along two fields to where the path emerges onto the road via a low ladder stile. Turn left along the road and, after 175m, go right at the next fork.

Just beyond the buildings on the left, at Bowersyke, is a double gateway at the entrance to Greenholme farm. Go up the steep and winding drive to the farm, and on approaching the farmyard go through a field gate on the right below the buildings and across the field to another gate. Continue gently descending across another field, and then contour along towards the middle of the wood ahead. The indistinct path goes down through the wood to a wooden stile in a fence, and then follows another fence on the right, above a field. On reaching a facing gate, go through, cross a small beck, and continue along the bottom of the next field. Do not go into the farmyard at Grassrigg, but continue straight ahead over another stile in a fence. Keep following the wall or fence on the right for another 600m to reach the A684 again at a stile opposite a cottage. From here it is about 300m up the road to the layby and the parked car.

Walk No. 13

RIVER MINT AND THE FLANKS OF BENSON KNOTT

12-13.6km (7½ -8½ miles)

This walk from Kendal follows the lower reach of the attractive River Mint, and affords fine views from the slopes of Benson Knott, one of the prominent high points surrounding the town.

Start the walk from Mint Bridge on the A6, close to the entrance of Morrison's superstore, which has a cafe where you can get light meals. If you are walking from the centre of Kendal, you can take an urban footpath through the industrial estate of Mintsfeet. The footpath starts at the footbridge over the railway in Beezon Road, and runs via Mintsfeet Road and Mintsfeet Road North to join the River Kent at the large lagoon or gravel trap close to its confluence with the River Mint. This is a good place to see water fowl, and is only 500m downstream from the main start at Mint Bridge.

Follow the river path up the Mint, alongside the perimeter fence of Morrison's, formerly the site of the Westmorland County Show Ground. After about 1.2km (¾ mile), the path emerges by a stile onto the Meal Bank road, where turn left. Follow the road past, but not over, the fine stone arch of Laverock Bridge, continuing past a farm and uphill to where a narrow path on the left, beside a concrete road grit bunker, goes through the wood, with a fence on its left. Where you reach the minor road at Meal Bank, a short cut leads uphill to the Appleby road railway bridge (see map).

However, to follow the full route, turn left down the road, then bear right in the centre of the former mill hamlet, with a terrace of white houses on the right, and go straight ahead between outbuildings to cross the drive of a new house. Keep round the edge of the garden and uphill beside the hedge to a stile into a field. Continue through the opening at the top of the field and along the track above Meal Bank wood, with the Mint traversing a moraine below.

After 300m on this track, where it descends steeply through a derelict gateway towards a minor stream, leave the track and go diagonally up the field to a stile in the hedge at the top, where, looking back, there is a good view of the Haweswater aqueduct. Over the stile, bear half right to go between the top of the hill and the railway, and through a gateway in a broken wall. A farm track soon starts, and leads to a gate onto a minor road (where you join the short cut from Meal Bank). Turn left and go up to the Appleby road, turning left again to cross the railway bridge, and continue 100m to the old Toll House on the left.

Next follows the main climb of the walk. Just past the Toll House go up a signposted track on the right, past a solitary barn, continuing up beside the wall on the right. Where the track leaves the wall and becomes faint,

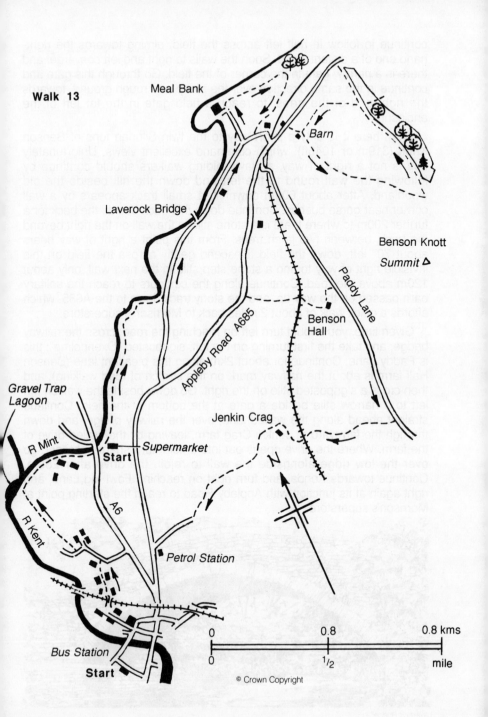

Walk 13

Meal Bank

Barn

Laverock Bridge

Benson Knott

Summit △

Paddy Lane

*Gravel Trap
Lagoon*

Appleby Road A685

Benson
Hall

R Mint

Jenkin Crag

Supermarket

Start

N

A6

R Kent

Petrol Station

Bus Station

Start

| 0 | | 0.8 | | 0.8 kms |

| 0 | | 1/2 | | mile |

© Crown Copyright

continue to follow it, half left across the field, aiming towards the right-hand end of a distant wood. Soon the walls to right and left converge, and there is a narrow gate in the corner of the field. Go through this gate and continue in the same direction over the steep and rough ground, towards the right end of the trees, to reach a field gate in the far left of the enclosure.

From here it is only a short way to the twin Silurian tops of Benson Knott (319m or 1046ft), which command excellent views. Unfortunately this is not a right of way, so law-abiding walkers should continue by following the wall round to the left and down the hill beside the old woodland. After about 600m downhill, a small track appears by a wall corner near gorse bushes. Continue down this track beside the beck for a further 200m to where there is a stone stile in the wall on the right beyond the beck, between two larch trees. From this point a right of way bears about 70° left, down the field. Descend gently across the field on this invisible right of way to find a stone step stile in the next wall, only about 120m above the road. Continue along the contours to reach the solitary barn passed on the way up, and the stony track down to the A685, which affords a quick walk of about 2 miles back to Morrison's superstore.

Given time, you should turn left on reaching the road, cross the railway bridge, and take the first turning on the left, signposted "Oxenholme"; this is Paddy Lane. Continue for about 2km along this pleasant lane (Benson Hall farm is about the halfway mark on this stretch of road walking), and then cross a signposted stile on the right. Go down beside the wall on the left to a narrow stile beside a gate at the bottom of the field. Continue straight ahead along the walled lane, over the railway bridge, and down through the farmyard at Jenkin Crag farm, leaving by the walled drive of the farm. Where the drive opens out into a field, turn sharp right, and go over the low ridge alongside the wall to rejoin the drive after 250m. Continue towards Kendal and turn right on reaching Fowl Ing Lane, and right again at its junction with Appleby Road to reach the starting point at Morrison's superstore.

Laverock Bridge

Walk No. 14

THREE PASSES WALK   16km (10 miles)

In this walk, the gentler landscapes of limestone and Silurian rock in the south of our area give way to the rugged and precipitous mountain scenery associated with the Borrowdale volcanic series. This is a real mountain walk, and as such commands a certain respect. Bear in mind before attempting it that the temperature at 500m may be very different from that in the valleys. There may be ice on the fells even in spring and autumn, and there are few more frightening things than to find yourself on an icy and precipitous path without a proper grip on your soles. Ordinary walking boots are not adequate in these circumstances.

The walk crosses three passes in the eastern fells, and involves a total of 850m (2,800 feet) of ascent. It follows part of the ancient packhorse route from Kendal to Penrith, by crossing the Gatescarth Pass from Longsleddale to Mardale. Next it crosses Nan Bield Pass to the Kentmere valley. Finally it follows the bridle track from Stile End to Sadgill. The passes, though high, are relatively easy, and cover some of the finest mountain scenery in eastern Lakeland.

You can park near the bridge at Sadgill (GR 483056), which you reach by taking the Shap road (A6) from Kendal for about 6km (4 miles), and then turning left at the sign "Longsleddale 4½". 8km (5 miles) of winding road lead to the last settlement in the valley, the hamlet of Sadgill.

From the bridge, take the quarry road leading up the east side of the valley to the top of the Gatesgarth Pass. The impressive mountain scenery that is typical of this walk becomes evident as the path climbs between Goat Scar on the left and Buckbarrow Crag on the right. The rocky gorge of the River Sprint, with its cascades and pools, adds interest to the climb, which Mr Wainwright described as "eminently suitable for nonagenarians".

Follow the quarry road until it ends soon after passing through the second gate. From this point, a narrower path climbs to the right, away from the wall. The lower section has been reconstructed, but higher up the path is badly eroded and can be very wet in poor weather. Follow the path to the summit of the pass at 580m (1,900 feet).

As you descend into Mardale, the High Street range dominates the view in front, the steep, craggy northern face of Harter Fell appears on the left, and the gentler slopes of Branstree rise on the right. You soon reach the head of Mardale, with a good view over Haweswater. About 80m before the car park, look for a signpost "Bridleway Kentmere". Take this path, which leads to the top of the Nan Bield pass. After the first 50m across the grass, there is a well-trodden path all the way.

The going is rougher and the climbing is harder, but the magnificent scenery, especially the waterfalls and cascades, make it all well worth the

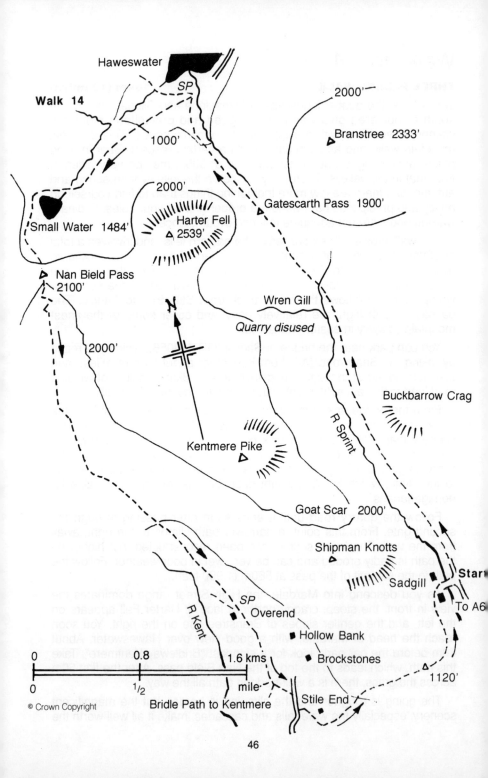

Haweswater

Walk 14

SP

2000'

1000'

Branstree 2333'

2000'

Gatescarth Pass 1900'

Small Water 1484'

Harter Fell
2539'

Nan Bield Pass
2100'

Wren Gill

Quarry disused

2000'

N

Buckbarrow Crag

R Sprint

Kentmere Pike

Goat Scar 2000'

Shipman Knotts

Sadgill

Start

To A6

SP
Overend

Hollow Bank

Brockstones

Stile End

1120'

R Kent

0   0.8   1.6 kms

0   ½   mile

© Crown Copyright

Bridle Path to Kentmere

effort. After you have passed the tarn of Small Water, a last determined effort will take you to the shelter at the top of the third highest and sharpest pass in the Lake District. Looking north east, the view includes Cross Fell and the northern Pennines, while to the south you may see to Morecambe Bay and the Bowland hills. The shapely cone of Ill Bell rises above the Kentmere reservoir.

The descent from Nan Bield starts with a series of steep zigzags, but the angle gradually decreases, and a pleasant kilometre or two of moorland walking leads down the valley of the River Kent. The path stays high on the mountainside until the valley broadens beyond the reservoir. From this point it continues in the same direction while descending gently towards the floor of the valley to reach the road at Overend farm.

Go through the left-hand one of two gates, and up the metalled road. Look for a signpost "Bridleway" on the right, just beyond a sheep enclosure. Here bear right along a grassy track, go through a gate, and then follow the partially-metalled track left and uphill. Pass through a gate to reach a minor road at a signpost "Bridleway to Mardale". Here turn right and follow the road for about 180m to a lane on the left with a signpost to Longsleddale. Take this lane to the top of the third pass. The route is obvious all the way, and from the top a steady descent leads to the bridge at Sadgill, and so completes the walk.

Walk No. 15

KENDAL TO BOWNESS-ON-WINDERMERE   16.8km (10½ miles)
VIA UNDERBARROW

For anyone visiting Kendal before a walking holiday in the Lakes, here is an opportunity to limber up before going onto the high fells. The route is pleasantly varied, and there is transport at the other end, including ferries up and down the lake (details from the Tourist Information Centre in Kendal Town Hall at the start of the walk). The walk should take about five hours.

From the Town Hall, go up Allhallows Lane and Beast Banks, forking left at the green to go up Brigsteer Road. Follow the road over the bypass, and then look for a stone stile in the wall on the right, signposted to Scout Scar. Cross the old racecourse and follow the track through a kissing gate and over a stone stile. (If a bull grazing with the herd on the racecourse looks menacing, continue along the road to the third iron field gate (padlocked), and go up the fell to rejoin the route beyond the kissing gate and stile.) Continue following the track from the stile until you reach the edge of the escarpment (about 3.5 km from the Town Hall).

Where a large cairn marks the junction with the path along the edge of the scar, go diagonally across to join a narrower path, steeply descending

Beast Banks, Kendal

towards Barrowfield farm below. Follow the track beside the field to the farm, where waymarks point the way around the farm buildings to the drive beyond. Here turn right and follow the sign on an electricity pole pointing down the hill to a stile into a wood. Carry on through the wood and across a field to a high stone stile leading into a larger wood. Follow the path between the trees, and when you reach a forestry road continue in the same direction, along the waymarked path towards Garth Row Lane. On emerging from the wood at a gate, continue straight across the field, skirting around the left of an old orchard to reach a track going right, past the houses and and out into the lane.

Turn left along the lane for a short distance to where, at the first bend, a short track leads into a field. Pass the small barn,, and then turn right and head for a stile and gate in the far left corner of the field. Beyond the stile and gate, aim half left to another stile in a short stretch of wall. Cross the clapper bridge and bear slightly right to reach a stile into a narrow lane. Turn left along the lane, past Tullythwaite House and the adjoining bungalow, and then go up a signposted drive to Rockyfield. Follow the waymarked path around the far end of the garden (not in the field) to emerge onto another road. Turn right and follow the road to Underbarrow and the Punch Bowl Inn, where you can get food and drink (1½-2 hours from Kendal).

Continue up the road signposted to Crook and Staveley, opposite the inn. Just past the first bend, take the side road on the right, continuing along this road where it bends left in front of a farm gate, and ignoring footpath arrows to right and left. Turn right at the T-junction in front of "The Barn" to reach the road near Underbarrow church. Go up the lane beside the church, and just past the first house on the right, the old vicarage, follow the sign on the left across two fields and a footbridge to reach the road. Turn right along the road and take the second turning on the left, a track up beside a wood. At the end of the enclosed woodland, cross a stile and go up the steep bank, through bracken.

At the crest of the hill, a wide view opens up and the route continues half left, following an indistinct cart track going parallel to the wall on the left for about 500m across rough pasture. Ignore the gate in the wall on the left and continue to a tall ladder stile near a wall corner. This stile crosses the boundary between Underbarrow and Crook parishes. Keep on, with the wall and a small beck now on the right, to another stile, from where a good track continues in the same direction to the drive of Low Fold farm. Go up the drive and cross the farmyard to leave by a gate just to the right of a small stone outbuilding.

Follow this farm track as it crosses two fields, swings left along the contours, and goes through a gate beside a small quarry, giving fine views of the Lakeland fells. Where the track peters out at the entrance to a field, keep straight across the slope to a stile near the bottom corner of

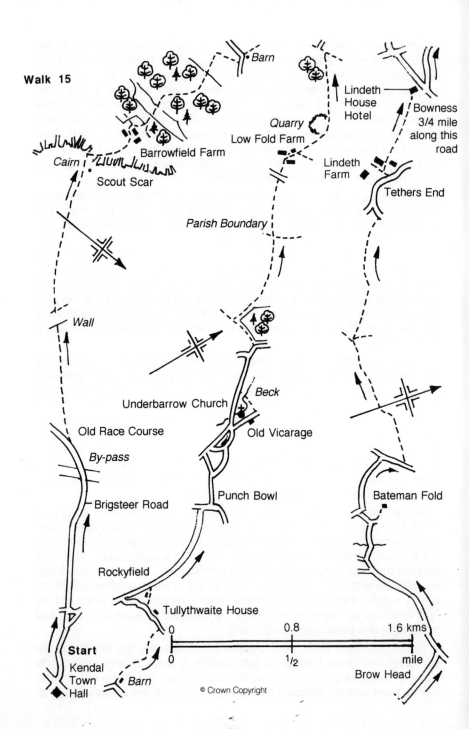

Walk 15

Barn

Barrowfield Farm

Cairn

Scout Scar

Quarry
Low Fold Farm

Lindeth
House
Hotel

Bowness
3/4 mile
along this
road

Lindeth
Farm

Tethers End

Parish Boundary

Wall

Beck

Underbarrow Church

Old Vicarage

Old Race Course

By-pass

Brigsteer Road

Punch Bowl

Bateman Fold

Rockyfield

Tullythwaite House

Start
Kendal
Town
Hall

Barn

Brow Head

0   0.8   1.6 kms

0   1/2   mile

© Crown Copyright

some rough woodland, and then cross the next field diagonally to a track at the opposite corner. After leaving this field, turn sharp right down a metalled track to Brow Head.

Turn left along the winding minor road from Brow Head, and follow it for about 1.6km (1 mile), bearing right at the signpost to Crosthwaite and again at the signpost to Winster. Ignore the drive to Bateman Fold on the right and a narrow lane on the left, and on reaching a T-junction with a bigger road, turn right. After 250m go up a walled track that doubles back on the left. Follow it for about 800m (½ mile), over the crest of the hill, and as it descends round a right-hand bend, go through a field gate on the right, close to a rocky outcrop. Ignore the good track going straight ahead, and immediately go diagonally downhill on rough tracks through bracken, aiming for the ladder stile that you will shortly see crossing the wall at the bottom of the hill. After crossing the stile, go straight across the field, keeping parallel to the wall on the left and passing right of a high-fenced enclosure, to reach an unfenced road going left to a cattle grid and leading onto another road.

Turn right along the road for 250m to a footpath sign at Lindeth Farm. Follow the sign to the left and, just before the sign to Tethers End, cross a stone stile on the right and go uphill to pass just left of an interesting old galleried house and reach a gate into a field. Cross the field on the line of the electricity poles to a gate to the left of the wood, and then follow the wall on the left over the hill and down to a kissing gate in the left-hand corner. Continue on the fenced path beside a pond with exotic water fowl and, soon after emerging onto the drive, turn right onto a grassy path beside a wooden garage. This path descends steeply to emerge onto the main Crook-Bowness road at the entrance to the Lindeth House Hotel. Cross to the minor road opposite on the left, and follow it until it joins a major road leading to the centre of Bowness.

Walk No. 16

HUTTON ROOF CRAG AND THE LANCASTER CANAL

18.4km (11½ miles)

This walk starts at Holme church (GR 524788), crosses an attractive stretch of limestone upland between Farleton Fell and Hutton Roof Crags, descends through pleasant farming country south of Burton-in-Kendal, and returns to Holme via the towpath of the Kendal and Lancaster Canal. It is a walk of considerable interest and variety, with magnificent views of the Lakeland fells, the Howgills, and the Pennines. Some short sections through farmyards can be very muddy.

There is a car park opposite Holme church. Beside the car park is North Road, signposted to Farleton and Kendal. Go along this road for 130m, and just before the school turn right along a road that leads between playing fields to the canal towpath. Follow the towpath to the left, under three bridges, until it comes to a road; here go to the right under the motorway to reach the A6070. Turn right and walk about 400m to a large farm on the left (Holme Park farm).

Immediately beyond the farmhouse, turn left onto a bridleway that leads up between Holme Park quarry (fortunately hidden from view) on the right and Holmepark Fell on the left. At the top of the hill continue straight ahead until the track turns left near the end of the quarry. At this point bear slightly right along a grassy track that leads to a metal field gate. Pass through the gate and take the upper path, bearing north-east (half-left) over open heath, to reach a second metal gate after about 400m. Go through the gate and cross the field to a conspicuous ladder stile near a gate in the wall opposite. Climb the stile (or go through the gate) and continue straight ahead, crossing a farm track and following the line of an overhead cable to reach a gate at a wall corner.

Go through the gate to a road, cross the stile on the other side, and follow the obvious path beyond it. This path leads over the fell through bracken and juniper bushes to a height of 260m. From the top, there is a magnificent panoramic view of all the South Lakeland fells from Black Combe in the west to High Street and the Shap and Howgill Fells to the north; Ingleborough is prominent to the east. Beyond the top, the path swings left and then right to skirt the limestone crags, and then descends steeply to the village of Hutton Roof (also visited on Walk No. 18).

Turn right down the village street to the telephone kiosk. Here turn right and go straight ahead up the farmyard to a lane that leads to Park Wood nature reserve. (There is a temporary diversion at this point, to avoid an unsafe building. Instead of entering the farmyard, continue a further 60m along the road and go over a ladder stile on the right. Cross the field, bearing slightly left towards a waymark post, and walk up the grassy bank

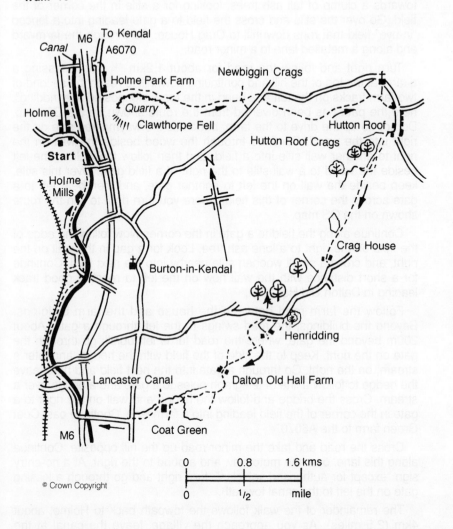

To Kendal
A6070

Canal M6

Holme Park Farm

Newbiggin Crags

Holme

Quarry

Clawthorpe Fell

Hutton Roof

Hutton Roof Crags

Start

Holme Mills

Crag House

Burton-in-Kendal

Henridding

Lancaster Canal

Dalton Old Hall Farm

M6

Coat Green

© Crown Copyright

0	0.8	1.6 kms

0	½	mile

and through a hole in the wall to join the lane at an entrance to the Park Wood nature reserve. Turn left along the lane.)

At the second nature reserve sign, leave the main track and go through the gate into the reserve. Keep straight ahead to a stile in the wall at the end of the reserve, and then bear half-right to a small clapper bridge over a beck. Continue straight ahead, climbing slowly, to reach and follow an old hedge and outcrops on the right to a gate next to a sheep pen. Go through the gate and continue along the upper boundary of the next field towards a clump of tall ash trees, looking for a stile in the corner of the field. Go over the stile and cross the field to a gate leading into a fenced "in-bye" field that runs downhill to Crag House. Go through the farmyard and along a metalled lane to a minor road.

Turn right and follow the road for about 1.2km (¾ mile), passing a quarry at the top of the hill and continuing downhill to reach the second of two farm tracks on the left at a bend in the road, signposted "Henridding"; here the path has been diverted from the route shown on the OS map. Do not go up the drive to the farm, but cross the waymarked stile on the right into the wood. Continue through the wood beside the wall on the right to another wall stile into a field, and then follow the wall on the left beside the wood to a wall stile to the right of a field gate. Over this stile, keep beside the wall on the left to another gate, and then bear left to a gate across the corner of this field, where you turn right to join the route shown on the OS map.

Continue along the field to a gate in the corner. Now follow the edge of the field on the right to a lone ash tree. Look for a gap in the wall on the right, and cross a small wooden stile nearby into the next field. Continue for a short distance with the wall now on the left to reach a good track leading to Dalton Old Hall farm.

Follow the farm road between the house and the farm buildings. Beyond the buildings, the road swings to the left through a gate. About 200m beyond the gate, where the road turns left uphill, go through the gate on the right. Keep to the side of the field with the hedge, and later a stream, on the right. Go through a gate into the next field and here leave the hedge to follow a line of telegraph poles to a gate and a bridge over a stream. Cross the bridge and follow the hedge and wall on the right to a gate in the corner of the field leading into a farm lane. Continue past Coat Green farm to the A6070.

Cross the road and take the minor road up the hill opposite. Continue along this lane, over the motorway, and around to the right. At a no-entry sign "except for authorised vehicles", turn right and go through a kissing gate on the left to the canal towpath.

The remainder of the walk follows the towpath back to Holme, about 4km (2.5 miles). As you approach the village, leave the canal at the bridge where the canal banks have been concreted. Go up the concrete steps, turn left, and follow the road back to the car park.

Walk No. 17

THE SEVEN CHURCHES OF KIRKBY LONSDALE (1)

19.2km (12 miles)

This walk and the next complement each other, and together they include visits to all the six daughter churches of the mother church at Kirkby Lonsdale . The walk is basically a valley walk, so any climbing is quite gentle, and there are several stretches of road walking that allow good progress. Refreshments are available at the Pheasant Inn, Casterton, the Barbon Inn, and another just off the route, 500m north of Middleton church.

If travelling by car, park on the east side of Devil's Bridge at Kirkby Lonsdale (GR 617783); otherwise walk from the town centre via Jingling Lane and the footpath past the cricket ground to cross Devil's Bridge. A lane starts from the extreme north-eastern corner of the car park on the east side of the A683 Sedbergh road. Go up here for a few metres and cross a stone step stile at the first bend in the lane. Go up the middle of the field and between caravans. On reaching the caravan-site road, bear left, then left again to go through a hedge, where turn right, over a cattle grid to reach a hedged bridleway.

Turn left along the bridleway for a few metres to cross a stile on the right, continuing across the overflow campsite and up the field beside the wall to where, just beyond a hedge junction, there is another stile. Go diagonally up the next field and pass a hedge corner on the right to descend to a gate, hidden at first, which leads into another hedged bridleway. Continue up the bridleway and subsequent metalled road to turn left at the next junction. Go along this road, heading north, for about 400m. (¼ mile) to the crossroads, and then turn left again. After about 100m take the signposted kissing gate on the right and go diagonally across to a stile. Continue in this direction across two more stiles to reach a narrow path going round the left of the houses, and emerge onto the main road near a filling station. Turn right along the road; you will soon find CASTERTON church.

After a possible visit to the church, follow the lane up behind it, past the school. After going under the old railway bridge, cross over Wandales Lane, which is on the line of the former Roman road; Casterton, as its name implies, was a Roman settlement. Go up the lane to Langthwaite and, just past all the buildings, go over a ladder stile on the left and follow the field boundary on the left above the buildings to another ladder stile. (This path has recently been diverted away from the buildings.) Now go gradually downhill to the left-hand one of two gates in the far left corner of the field near Hole House. Continue along the narrow field to reach Fell Garth.

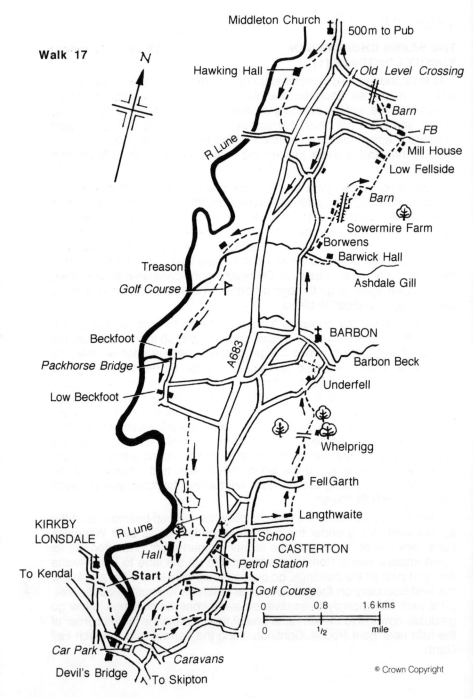

Walk 17

Middleton Church

500m to Pub

Hawking Hall

Old Level Crossing

Barn

R Lune

FB

Mill House

Low Fellside

Barn

Sowermire Farm

Borwens

Treason

Barwick Hall

Golf Course

Ashdale Gill

Beckfoot

BARBON

Barbon Beck

Packhorse Bridge

A683

Underfell

Low Beckfoot

Whelprigg

Fell Garth

Langthwaite

KIRKBY
LONSDALE

R Lune

School

CASTERTON

Hall

To Kendal

Petrol Station

Start

Golf Course

0   0.8   1.6 kms

0   ½   mile

Caravans

Car Park

Devil's Bridge

To Skipton

© Crown Copyright

56

Keeping right of the farm, go through a small wooden gate and then over a stile onto the road. Continue through the gate opposite, and follow the wall to a gate near an electricity transformer pole. Go on in the same northerly direction through several gates and gateways, and across the parkland of Whelprigg House, whose driveway you soon cross via a stile and a gate. Continue in the same direction, aiming for the field gate seen ahead. Through the gate, bear left on the track, but do not go as far as the farmyard of Low Bank; instead, cross a stile on the right next to a field gate. Cross the corner of the field to a wicket gate, and then follow the wall to a road. Go right along the road, to leave it again after 200m at Underfell, by keeping straight on past the outbuildings where the road turns sharp right. Across the yard, take the right-hand gate. After the next gate, go down the bridleway for a few metres to another stile, which leads across the field to BARBON church.

Turn left to go through the village, and then take the first turning right to resume going north. Stay on this road for about 1km (¾ mile). Just after an access road on the right (to Barwick Hall), the road crosses Ashdale Gill, beyond which a stile on the right leads to Borwens farm. Go through the farm in front of the farmhouse, to continue in the same direction via a gate straight ahead. Aim for the right-hand end of a belt of trees, where a plank bridge crosses a small beck and leads via a stile to a road.

Turn right on the road to Sowermire Farm, where turn right again to go under the old railway bridge. Immediately afterwards turn left and walk alongside the old line until the double fencing ends. Here turn diagonally right and make for a gateway beyond the electricity line. Turn right to go past a barn, and follow the wall and fence round two sides of the field to reach a gateway in the far right corner. Then follow the wall on the right across two more fields, and go through a field gate on the right at the end of the second (near a ruined step stile).

Go up the hill to the right of the barn, and on to Low Fellside farm. Cross the field above the buildings (probably much churned up by horses) to another stone step stile. Now bear slightly right, uphill, towards the buildings soon seen ahead, aiming for a gateway left of the barn. Through the gate, to avoid boggy ground bear right towards the ruined cottage, and you will find a track leading to a footbridge over Millhouse Beck. Looking up the beck from the bridge you can see Middleton Fell straight ahead; this is the highest point of the walk.

Cross the stone stile beyond the bridge to reach the farm drive, and follow it down for about 100m to a gap stile at the end of the wall on the right. Now go diagonally left to a stile beside a gate, and continue in the same direction, under the electricity line, to a gap stile at the junction of a fence and wall. Keep in the same direction to another gap stile, then, very soon, a gate, and then another stile in a short length of wall ahead. Continue on to cross a wooden stile in the fence beside Ellers farm drive.

Devil's Bridge, Kirkby Lonsdale

Go left down the drive and over the old railway level crossing. On reaching the tarmac road, continue straight ahead over the crossroads to meet the A683, and turn right along it to reach MIDDLETON church.

The route continues by going through the gate off the main road just to the south of the church. Go diagonally across the field and through the left-hand gate. (There is an old Roman milestone on the hill on the left, close to two trees.) Aim for the bottom of the wooded slope ahead, where a stony and often muddy track leads to Hawking Hall farm.

Go through the farmyard and along the lane ahead (Low Lane), and when the lane turns left continue ahead on the dirt lane (very wet at times). At the end, turn left on the side road, and cross the main road to a stile. (You can omit the following loop by taking the main road right for about 1km (¾ mile), but the road is quite busy and the loop is rewarding for the splendid views of the Middleton fells.)

Follow the hedge up to another gap stile, continue beside the hedge or wall to a third stile, and then cross the middle of the next field to a wide gate. Turn right on the road (High Road) and, after about 500m, just past Applegarth, turn right into Betweengates Lane. Stay on this lane for about 800m (½ mile) until you reach the main road. Turn left for about 50m, and then take the farm road, opposite, to Treasonfield. Beyond the farm, keep to the hedged lane for about 1.5km (1 mile), passing Kirkby Lonsdale's golf course, until you arrive at High Beckfoot, where there is an interesting old packhorse bridge over Barbon Beck.

Continue along the lane (Lowfields Lane), ignoring the broad turning off left. Just beyond Low Beckfoot, with its pheasant rearing pens, go under an arched bridge and then follow the road left alongside a wooded ravine. At the end of the wood, take the second of two field gates on the right and follow the wall across two fields to a gate in the corner of the second, and then follow the wall on the left. Where the wall ends, aim for a high ladder stile, and then a wooden stile at the corner of the wood. Follow the fence along above the wood to an iron kissing gate in the corner, which leads to a track through the wood.

On emerging from the wood, cross the field to a stile into another wood straight ahead, with a rough, wet track leading over a beck. After crossing the beck, bear right up the hill, and alongside the wood on the right to reach a waymarked kissing gate leading into a field. Continue, to reach the big house, Casterton Hall, where the waymarks show the route straight through the buildings. Cross the drive to an iron kissing gate, and then use the fenced path through the park to reach the main road.

Turn left along the main road, taking great care around the bend, and after about 150m go up the signposted bridleway on the right (Laitha Lane). When it forks, go right, and follow the lane back to the caravan site, or to its junction with a metalled lane, where turn right to reach the car park.

Walk No. 18

THE SEVEN CHURCHES OF KIRKBY LONSDALE (2)

18.4km (11½ miles)

This walk complements the previous one, visiting the remaining three daughter churches, at Hutton Roof, Lupton, and Mansergh. together with the mother church at Kirkby Lonsdale. It is best avoided after continuous rain, as some of the green lanes are apt to flood, and there are many hay and silage fields to be crossed, which can be a very wetting experience before the grass is cut. There is no need to go round the edges of these fields to avoid trampling the crop, but remember to keep in single file on the lines of the paths. The only refreshments obtainable on the route are crisps, sweets, etc. from the Post Office at Hutton Roof, which is still open at the time of writing.

From the Market Square in Kirkby Lonsdale, go south along the main street and cross the A65 to the Whittington road opposite. About 200m along here, just past the telephone exchange, go through an iron kissing gate on the right and climb the hill towards the wood on the left. Continue alongside the wood until you are just beyond the summit of the hill. Then go left through the wood along a short, walled lane, turn right, and continue with the wood now on your right to reach Wood End farm via an iron kissing gate between the wood and the cow shed. Go down the farm drive to reach a road.

Bear left along the road for a short distance, and then fork right up a side road to High Biggins, keeping straight ahead through the hamlet. About 300m beyond the road junction at High Biggins, go through a gap stile on the left, signposted "Kilner Foot", at the entrance to a caravan site. Head at 45° across the field to another gap stile. The blue arrows indicate that you are on part of the Limestone Link, a medium-distance path from Arnside to Kirkby Lonsdale, but it is not a bridleway despite the colour of the arrows. Continue along the second field, aiming about 30° away from the hedge on the right, to reach another waymarked stile at the far side of the field.

Beyond the stile go straight ahead along the left side of the rough strip of grass and reach a stile and field gate. Now go diagonally left down the field to a gate, continuing on the same line to the bottom of the hill and the left-hand one of two gates. Then follow the line of electricity poles up the hill to find a stile close to the corner of the field. Keep in the same direction, following the electricity poles to another stone step stile. Hutton Roof Crags are ahead, with Farleton Knott over on the right, and Hutton Roof church in the middle distance. Over the stile, stay beside the wall on the left, down the hill, via a gate to a step stile in the bottom corner, leading into a green lane. Follow the lane to the road. Turn left along the

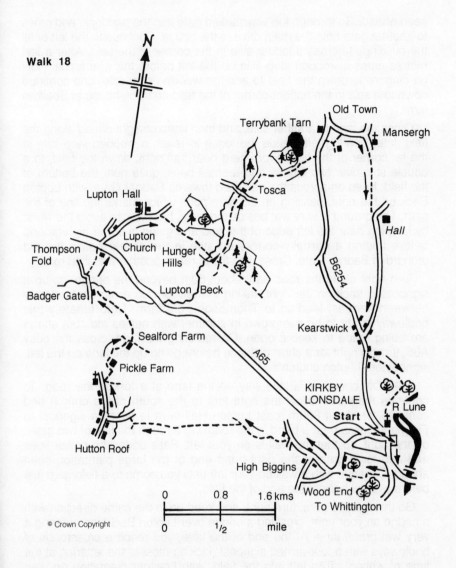

© Crown Copyright

road into Hutton Roof, and then right on the main street, past the Post Office, to reach HUTTON ROOF church.

Two footpaths (no doubt much used by worshippers in days gone by) start at the stile opposite the church gate, but only the one to Gale Barn is signposted. Your route follows a right of way that bears left beyond the stile and skirts round the left of the rocky outcrops to reach Pickle Farm, seen ahead. Go through the waymarked gate into the paddock, and cross to another gate onto the main drive to the house. Continue to the left of all the buildings to cross a ladder stile in the corner of the field. After a few metres cross a wooden step stile on the left before the wire fence. Now go diagonally down the field to another wooden step stile, and continue down to a stile in the bottom corner of the field near the house at Sealford farm.

Cross the lane to another stile, and then keep straight ahead along the field, later bearing left beside the fence to reach a wooden step stile in the far corner of the field. From here bear half right, down the field, to a double stile over two fences and a small beck, quite near the bottom of the field. Keep on across the next field towards Badger Gate, with Lupton Beck on the right, passing an old gate post, which marks the line of the path. The ground is very wet beside the beck, but you can avoid the worst by keeping near the left edge of the field and going over the high ground before finding a partially-concealed stile in the corner below the old orchard of Badger Gate. Cross the stile to reach another metalled road.

Turn right along the road and, about 50m beyond the bridge, go up a signposted track on the right, taking the left fork up a narrow bridleway between hedges, leading to Thompson Fold farm. Unfortunately this bridleway is apt to be overgrown in summer with nettles etc., but efforts are being made to keep it open. On reaching the farm, cross the busy A65, turning right for a short distance before going up the lane on the left, signposted "Lupton church".

LUPTON church is a little way up the lane at a fork in the road. To continue the walk, follow the right fork to the south of the church and continue for about 800m, past Lupton Hall farm to reach a signpost to Fleet and Tosca near a bend in the road. Go through the first of two gates on the right, so that the wall is on your left. Pass under the power lines and aim for a gate at the right-hand end of the large plantation seen ahead. Continue with a wall on your left until you come to a field gate just before a small beck at the end of the field.

Go through the gate, turn right, and keep on in the same direction with a hedge on your right, crossing a bridge over Lupton Beck and entering a very wet green lane. At the end of the lane, you reach a crossroads of bridleways with a four-armed signpost (lacking most of the lettering at the time of writing). Turn left into the field, with Lowther plantation on your right, and go diagonally across the field towards a gateway in the hedge ahead, and then diagonally left to a gate near the beck. Continue with the beck on your left, skirting around the base of the hill on the right, and then going over its shoulder to reach a road at Tosca farm.

Turn right in front of the farm and, at the end of the buildings, follow a sign to the left to Old Town, going through a field gate beyond the Dutch barn. Beyond the gate, turn sharp left along a cart track to a gate, and

Hutton Roof Church

then continue with a fence on your right to another gate. Now turn sharp right up the hill beside the wall to another gate. On reaching a corner beside the wood ahead, turn right through a field gate, and then left along the edge of the wood to a ladder stile. After negotiating this precipitous stile, bear left around the shoulder of the hill, with Terrybank Tarn on the left (seen best from the top of the hill) to reach a track leading to two field gates in the corner of the field. Go through the left-hand gate and up the field, with the wood on your right, to a stile in the corner leading onto the B6254.

Turn left and go along the road for 250m, looking for a stone step stile on the right about 150m before the first buildings of Old Town. Cross the stile, where there is a fine view of Mansergh church and the Middleton and Barbon fells beyond. Follow the wall round to a waymarked stile in the wall near Hawkrigg, and over it another wall, descending to the drive in front of the farmhouse. Turn left down the drive to reach the road. Follow the road to the right for 400m to reach Mansergh old school and MANSERGH church close to it on the right.

Continue the walk past the church, through the gate, and on through a gateway in a hedge to reach a hedged lane at the next gate. Keep going along this fine green lane until it emerges onto a road near Mansergh Hall farm. Continue in the same direction, southwards along the road for about 1.5km (1 mile) until you get to Kearstwick, where you join the B6254 again at a T-junction.

Turn left, walk along the road for about 150m, and then follow a signpost to the left down a drive. Go through a waymarked iron kissing gate on the right, opposite the old barn, and along a narrow path to emerge shortly onto a dirt road via a stile. Underley Hall, now a school, is over to the left, beyond the fruit farm. When you reach a cross track near a stone bridge, keep straight ahead through an iron wicket gate, along beside the iron fence on the left, passing over another small stone bridge, and up a track into the wood. Follow the path through the wood, with the Lune below on the left, until you reach the mother church of KIRKBY LONSDALE.